CITIES OF THE BIBLICAL WORLD

Jericho

John R. Bartlett

Lecturer in Divinity, and
Fellow of Trinity College, Dublin

LUTTERWORTH PRESS
GUILDFORD, SURREY

CITIES OF THE BIBLICAL WORLD

General Editor:
Graham I. Davies, Lecturer in Divinity,
  Cambridge University

Other Titles:
Excavation in Palestine, Roger Moorey, Senior Assistant Keeper,
  Department of Antiquities, Ashmolean Museum, Oxford.
Qumran, Philip R. Davies, Lecturer in Biblical Studies, University
  of Sheffield.

In Preparation:
Beersheba and Arad, Graham I. Davies.
Ugarit (Ras Shamra), Adrian H. W. Curtis, Lecturer in Old
  Testament Studies, University of Manchester.

First published in 1982

ISBN 0–7188–2456–3

Set in 10/12 pt. Plantin
Phototypeset by Input Typesetting Ltd, London SW19 8DR
Printed and bound in Great Britain at
The Camelot Press Ltd, Southampton

Contents

List of Illustrations

Preface

This book is inevitably based on the work of a large number of travellers and scholars, and in particular on the work of a distinguished series of archaeologists – Condor, Sellin and Watzinger, Garstang, Pritchard and Kenyon, followed more recently by E. Netzer. Among these names (and others could be mentioned) it is hard not to single out that of Kathleen Kenyon, whose excavations at Tell es-Sultan crowned the earlier achievements of Sellin and Garstang and reached new heights of technical expertise in field archaeology. Her many publications on Jericho, whether on the popular or scholarly level, maintained a high standard of presentation and have been influential among scholars whose interests range from mesolithic to medieval periods in Palestinian history. It is impossible to write on Jericho without constantly referring to Kathleen Kenyon's work, and, as one who in 1962 worked in Jerusalem as one of her site supervisors and on a number of subsequent occasions received help and encouragement from her, I would like to take this opportunity of expressing my gratitude to a very great teacher. However, there is no point in simply re-presenting what Kenyon has already presented so well in *Digging up Jericho* and *The Archaeology of the Holy Land* (though the reader should know that the former book, published in 1957, does not represent the author's final views on several important matters), and in this book I have tried to avoid letting Kenyon's work dominate the presentation.

Although Jericho does not often appear in the Bible, its lasting fame has been assured by the stories of the collapse of its walls, the cleansing of its water by Elisha, the parable of the good Samaritan and the conversion of Zacchaeus. Of these four accounts, it is the first which is perhaps the most famous and it is certainly the one which provides the greatest difficulties for the historian. The biblical story of the collapse of Jericho's walls cries out for archaeological corroboration, and fifty years ago this was thought to have been found. It is now clear that there is no archaeological evidence to support the idea that the town of Jericho collapsed about the date usually assigned to Joshua, in the thirteenth century BC, and it is also clear from scholarly examination of the biblical account that Joshua 6 cannot be interpreted as a simple chronicle based on eye-witness report. These findings have produced a classic example of the difficulties of relating archaeological and literary evidence in the reconstruction of history. The archaeologist and the biblical scholar need each other, and in particular each needs to understand the meaning of the other's evidence. The interested but less professional student of such problems needs some help in interpreting the archaeological and biblical evidence, and the present book tries to meet that need. If the reader is forced to conclude, with Oscar Wilde, that truth is rarely pure and never simple, that may be no bad thing.

My thanks are due especially to the editor of this series, Graham Davies, for much good advice and careful attention to detail, and to Frances Shaw of Lutterworth Press for her editorial care.

Trinity College,
Dublin.

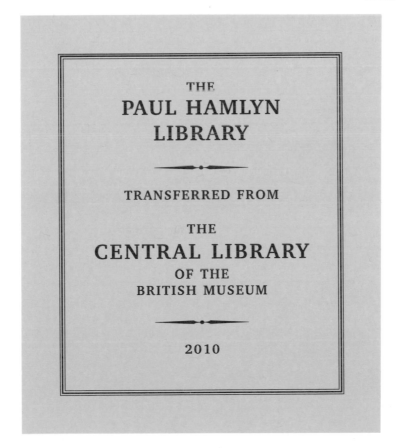

Chronological Table

BC	Jericho	Contemporaneous sites and peoples
10000		
–		Kebara
9500		
–	Natufian	Eynan
9000		
–	Proto-Neolithic	
8500		
–	PPNA	Wadi Fallah
8000		
–		
7500		Mureybet III
–	abandoned	
7000	PPNB	Beidha
–		
6500		Wadi Fallah
–		Tell Ramad, Munhata
6000		
–	abandoned	Beisamun
5500		Hagoshrim
–	PNA	Sha'ar Ha-golan, 'Yarmukian'
5000		Munhata 2B
–	PNB	Munhata 2A
4500		Byblos Middle Neolithic, W. Rabah
–	?abandoned	
4000	Ghassulian/ Chalcolithic	Teleilat Ghassul
–		
3500		
–	Proto-Urban	
3000	EB I	Egypt, Dynasty I
–	EB II	
2500	EB III	
–	(EB IV)	
2000	Intermediate EB-MB (MB I)	'Amorites'
1900	MB I (MB IIA)	Sesostris I, Sinuhe
1800	MB II (MB IIB-C)	Egypt, Middle Kingdom
1700		'Hyksos'
1600		
1500	?abandoned: LB I	Egypt, New Kingdom

8

			Israel
1400	LB II		
1300		Habiru	
1200	IA I		Joshua
1100			judges
1000		Philistines	David
900	IA II		divided monarchy
800	rebuilt by Hiel	Assyrian empire	
700			
600	IA III	Babylonian empire	exile
500		Persian empire	return
400	?abandoned		
300		Alexander the Great	
200		Ptolemies	
100		Seleucids	Maccabees
AD	Tulul abu el-ʿalaiq	Romans	Hasmonaeans
100			Herodians

1

'Like the garden of the Lord'

> And Lot lifted up his eyes, and saw that the Jordan valley was well watered everywhere, like the garden of the Lord (Gen. 13:10).

In this famous story, Abraham's nephew Lot, given the choice between the Palestinian hills and the Jordan valley, settled for the fertile valley. The story-teller quite deliberately pictures this valley as another Eden, a demi-paradise; the allusion to Genesis 2:10 is quite clear,

> A river flowed out of Eden to water the garden, and there it divided and became four rivers.

The lower Jordan valley round Jericho was a desirable place; it had plenty of fresh water, it was warm, and it was fertile. The Jewish historian Josephus in the first century AD called it *eudaimonestate*, 'most blessed'. But as the story-teller in Genesis and the historian Josephus both knew, the Jordan valley had its disadvantages. Genesis recalls the legends of the disaster that struck the cities of the plain,

> Then the LORD rained on Sodom and Gomorrah brimstone and fire from the LORD out of heaven; and he overthrew those cities, and all the valley, and all the inhabitants of those cities, and what grew on the ground. But Lot's wife behind him looked back, and she became a pillar of salt. And Abraham went early in the morning to the place where he had stood before the LORD; and he looked down toward Sodom and Gomorrah and toward all the land of the valley, and beheld, and lo, the smoke of the land went up like the smoke of a furnace (Gen. 19:24–28).

It has often been suggested that this biblical memory of the destruction of Sodom and Gomorrah may reflect comparatively recent geological events of the Upper Pleistocene or Holocene era, when the uplifting of Mount Sodom at the southern end of the Dead Sea caused the flooding of the plain. The rift valley of which the Dead Sea region forms part is an unstable area, and the position of the city of Jericho above geological fault lines may also have had something to do with the complaint of the men of Jericho to Elisha, 'Behold, the situation of the city is pleasant, as my lord sees; but the water

Plate 1   View of Tell es-Sultan and the oasis of Jericho from the north-west.

is bad, and the land is unfruitful'. This was apparently a temporary situation, and it has been suggested that it was caused by the contamination of the underground sources of the spring when earth movements brought the water into contact with strata bearing radio-active elements. Josephus also knows the disadvantages of the place, 'in summer the plain is burnt up, and the excessive drought renders the surrounding atmosphere pestilential: for it is wholly without water apart from the Jordan,' and apart from the spring at Jericho, which Josephus goes on to describe.

The land on either side of the Jordan was originally formed largely by a series of marine sediments deposited on the ancient sea of Tethys. At a later stage, after this basement had been covered with wind-blown sand from the desert to the southeast and water-laid limestone from the northwest, pressure from the north caused the contraction of the earth's surface beneath the sea of Tethys, and the folding of the edges of the landmass and its overlying deposits into mountains running in a southwest – northeast direction. It was the subsequent breaking up of the ancient landmass into several blocks which caused the fracture known as the 'rift valley', which is visible on the earth's surface from north Syria to central east Africa. The Jordan valley is a short section – and the deepest section – of this long fracture. The fracture may have been accompanied by the movement of the eastern block – Arabia – about 100 kms northward. Material along the line of the fracture sank relatively to the surrounding edges; the original surface of Upper Cretaceous marine sediment now lies deep below the present valley floor, covered by a 4000 metre thick layer of sediment washed down since the creation of the rift. The bed of the Jordan valley as we now know it is very largely the work of the comparatively recent Pleistocene period (*c.* 50,000–10,000 BC), in which, further north, there was a series of colder 'glacial' periods with warmer 'interglacial' periods between them. The glacial ice did not reach the rift valley, but its effects were seen in wet 'pluvial' and dry 'interpluvial' periods. The second of these pluvial periods filled the Jordan valley with water, turning it into a lake (the Lissan Lake) which stretched from the Sea of Galilee in the north to a point about 30 kms south of the present Dead Sea. In the following drier interpluvial period, the lake was reduced to two smaller lakes (the Sea of Galilee and the Dead Sea), connected by a channel which became the river Jordan. But the Lissan Lake left behind it clear signs of its presence in the thick deposits of marl and gypsum along the edges of the valley; at the southern end those deposits are about 150 metres thick.

For millennia, the river Jordan has been cutting its channel through the middle of these grey deposits left by the Lissan Lake. The large amount of silt suspended in the rapidly flowing river derives mainly from these deposits,

Map showing principal
sites mentioned.

Damascus•

T. Ramad•

•Ha-Goshrim

Beisamun)
•Ain Mallaha (Eynan)

Hazor•

Sepphoris•
Kh.Kerak•

Sheikh Ali•
Munhata•   •Gadara

W. Fallah
(Nahal
Oren)
          Megiddo•
Kebara•
          Taanach•
Strato's Tower•   Bethshan•

Kfar Monash•   T.el-Far'ah•   •Amathus

W. Rabah•   •Balata
          (Shechem)
          Alexandriume

          •Shiloh
W. Natul•   Phasaelis•
T.en-Nasbeh (Mizpah)•   Archelais•   Philadelphia•
Lydda•   •Ai Gilgal•   •'Araq el Emir
(Lod)   Gibeon•
Gezer•   T. es-Sultan (JERICHO)•   •Shittim
          Telellat Ghassul•
T Batashi•   •Jerusalem
          Beth-Hakkerem•   Hyrcania•   •Madeba
          Tekoa• Herodium•
          •el-
          Keilah• Khiam
•Ascalon   •Bethzur   •Machaerus
•T. ed-Duweir (Lachish)
•T. Ajjul
          T. Beit•
          Mirsim
          (Debir)   N. Mishmar•
          Arad• Masada•
•Sharuhen
Beersheba•

0   10   20   mls.

0   10   20   km.

Beidha
↓

Figure 1   Map showing principal sites mentioned.

and has helped create the ever changing meanders of the river, particularly south of the entry of the river Jabbok. On the silt banks of the meandering river has grown up the tropical undergrowth known as the *zor*, the Old Testament 'jungle of the Jordan' (Jer. 12:5; 49:19), the haunt of lions and wild boar. Jeremiah pictures God threatening Edom 'like a lion coming up from the jungle of the Jordan against a strong sheepfold'. A century ago H. B. Tristram noted that wild boar lived here and that 'about Jericho they are especially destructive, and when the barley crop is ripening, the husbandmen have to keep nightly watch to drive them away'. The river with its *zor* has cut down into the marl deposits, which now appear as a band of grey 'badlands' either side of the river, separating it from the terraces on the western and eastern edges of the Jordan valley. The soil of these terraces above the marl is the result of erosion from the hills above, and it has often become saline and unprofitable for agriculture without reclamation work.

The region around Jericho has been described by a recent geographer as 'arid plain'. Jericho itself, however, is sited on an alluvial fan washed down from the hills and watered by the three freshwater springs of ᶜAin es-Sultan, ᶜAin Duk, and ᶜAin Nuᶜeima. The rain which falls on the eastern slopes of the Judaean hills drains down towards the Dead Sea and Jordan valley, supplying an underground reservoir, and the springs are sited where the planes of rock along which the water flows reach the surface in the walls of the rift valley. Emerging at the springs, the water spreads eastward across the plain towards the Jordan. From ᶜAin es-Sultan (the spring beside the mound generally identified with ancient Jericho), the water falls 50 metres in about 1.5 kilometres, which means that its daily 30,000 or more cubic metres overflow spreads fairly fast in straight rather than meandering channels, which divide and today cover an area of about a thousand hectares. Most of this has been absorbed by the land via irrigation channels or evaporated before it reaches the Jordan. Just south of Jericho runs the perennial Wadi Qelt, its flow helped by two springs, ᶜAin el-Fawwar and ᶜAin Fara, which rise a few miles up the wadi west of Jericho. North of Jericho flows Wadi Nuᶜeima, running into the Jordan near the Allenby Bridge.

It is undoubtedly the combination of alluvial soil, a perennial freshwater spring, and permanent sunshine, that made Jericho an attractive place for settlement. The rainfall is almost negligible, totalling only 6.4 ins per annum, most of which falls between November and February. The average temperature for January is 59° F. and for August 88° F., though temperatures over 100° F. are not uncommon in summer. At the crest of the hills, 14 miles west of Jericho, the heat is tempered by the arrival each day about 10.00 a.m. of a light breeze from the sea. But the breeze does not reach the rift valley until mid-afternoon, and instead of cooling the hot rising air of

Plate 2   A 'bred-back' aurochs in the Tierpark, Hellabrunn, München.

the Jordan valley it is itself heated by it. The valley does not cool down until much later in the evening.

The traveller who stands on the Dead Sea shore is standing at the lowest known point of the earth's surface, 400 metres below sea-level. Jericho itself lies well above the level of the Dead Sea, at 230 metres below sea-level. The plant and animal life of this area is noticeably different from that of the rest of Palestine, and Tristram, in his *Flora and Fauna of Palestine*, published in 1884 as part of the monumental *Survey of Western Palestine*, noted the presence in the Jordan valley and plains round the Dead Sea of a number of species which derived from a southern, African, rather than a northern, Asian, background. The animal population of the Jericho region as elsewhere in the world has been severely reduced over the last century, and Tristram's survey of a century ago may be a much better guide to the animals of biblical times than any more recent list. It has the great merit of being derived from Tristram's personal observation as well as the observation of others.

It is not always appreciated that Jericho was about 10 kms or 6 miles west of the Jordan, and fish therefore may not have been eaten much at Jericho. But according to Tristram,

> The Jordan itself is alive with fish to its very exit, and carries by the rapidity of its current into the poisonous waters of the Dead Sea millions of fry, chiefly of bream, which are soon stupified and become the easy prey of birds which await them, while myriads of their carcases strew the shore near the mouth (*The Natural History of the Bible*, p. 286).

The sixth-century AD map on the floor of a church in Madeba shows fish swimming down the Jordan and turning back as they approach the Dead Sea. On land, snakes are common; the poisonous sand-viper (*echis arenicola*) hides among the stones by the shores of the Dead Sea. Geckos and lizards abound. Most of the Palestinian mammals appear in the area – bats, mice, the biblical coney (*hyrax syriacus*), hedgehogs and porcupines, and jackals. The wild boar have already been mentioned. Ibex are still seen; Tristram notes that he picked up an ibex horn near Jericho, and that he tried to rear a young one at Jericho, but failed. The place-names Beth-nimrah (Num. 32:3,6) and Numeirah at the southeastern end of the Dead Sea take their name from the leopard (Hebrew *namer*), and as recently as 1964 one was shot in the mountains south of Jericho. The Old Testament mentions lions in the Jordan valley (Jer. 49:19; Zech. 11:3), and a relief from ᶜArak el-Emir a few miles to the east across the Jordan shows a striding lion. Gazelles, sheep and goats have ranged here for millennia, and provided meat for Jericho from earliest times. Excavation has shown that the Jerichoans also fed on the aurochs (*bos primigenius*) (Plate 2), and the fox, at least in the early stages of the Neolithic period. The high cliffs and ravines of the Jordan valley and Dead Sea region are the natural habitat of a number of birds of prey – Tristram noted eagles in the Wadi Qelt and great owls in the caves of the Mount of Temptation above Jericho, together with a number of smaller birds 'more like those of India and Abyssinia, the Bulbul, Bushbabbler (*Crateropus chalybeus*), orange-winged Grakle (*amydus tristramii*), and especially the beautiful little sunbird (*Nectarinia oseae*)'. Particularly common were the rock pigeon in the Wadi Qelt and the palm turtle (*turtur senegalensis*) among the thorn bushes of the Jericho plain.

But Jericho is more famous for its flora than its fauna, clearly because Jericho is an oasis where useful plants can be cultivated. Jericho is known above all as 'the city of palms'. The story of Zacchaeus has made famous a certain sycamore tree at Jericho. Roman authors praised Jericho especially for the balm grown there. Jesus ben Sirach spoke in the second century BC of 'roses at Jericho'. The sons of the prophets at Gilgal in time of famine picked wild gourds and put them into their stew; on tasting it they cried out, 'There is death in the pot', and could not eat it. Jericho was known in biblical times for its plant life, both cultivated and wild; the oasis produced the former, and the surrounding salty plain the latter (see Figure 2).

Palm trees flourish in various places in Palestine. When Vespasian captured Judaea in AD 70 he celebrated the event with a coin which showed a captive sitting under a palm tree with the legend 'Iudaea capta'. The Hebrew word for palm is *tamar*, and it appears in a number of place-names. Hazazon-tamar (Gen. 14:7), perhaps the Tamar of Ezekiel 47:18f., is probably ᶜAin Husb at the south end of the Dead Sea, though 2 Chronicles 20:2

CITRULLUS COLOCYNTHUS.

Figure 2   Wild gourd (*citrullus colocynthus*).

identifies it with Engedi on the west coast of the Dead Sea, praised by Jesus ben Sirach for her date palms (Ecclus. 24:14). 'City of palms' appears as a name for Jericho at Deuteronomy 34:3, Judges 1:16; 3:12, 2 Chronicles 28:15. Josephus, in his *History of the Jewish War* against Rome (*Bellum Judaicum*), refers to the luxuriant palm-groves on the banks of the Jordan and to the palms irrigated by the spring at Jericho (*B.J.*4.455,468, Loeb ed.),

> Of the date-palms watered by it [the spring] there are numerous varieties differing in flavour and medicinal properties; the richer species of this fruit when pressed under foot emit copious honey, not much inferior to that of bees, which are also abundant in this region.

Tristram says that palm trees were reported as scarce at Jericho a century before his time, but that he discovered one wild palm with a clump of small ones on the edge of the stream just below the modern village. The *Survey of Western Palestine* (1883), quoting a report dated 1874, similarly refers to one solitary survivor growing 'close to the tower of er Riha'. Palms need attention if they are to be of much value. The female tree, which bears the fruit, must be pollinated from the male tree, and date-growers must therefore tend some male trees among the female trees of the plantation. The decline of the palms round Jericho was probably because the male trees had been left to grow outside the plantations, and had decayed. The situation appears to have changed, however, for there are plenty of palms in Jericho today. The date palm was used at least as early as Middle Bronze age Jericho, as tomb finds have shown; a bag and several woven objects were made from date-palm leaves. Evidence that dates were eaten was found at Teleilat Ghassul, a fourth millennium BC site just across the Jordan from Jericho. According to Tristram,

> It is a common saying among the Arabs that the Palm has as many uses as there are days in the year. In the oases, where it is the principal tree, every part of it is utilized. Besides its employment for building purposes, a pleasant drink is made from its juice; wine is distilled from its sap, and a spirit is fermented from it. The crown of barren trees is boiled as a vegetable; sugar is manufactured from the syrup; mats, baskets, and all sorts of utensils are manufactured from its leaves; horses are fed on the fruit-stalks, and camels on the pounded stones (*The Natural History of the Bible*, p. 386).

The sycamore tree that Zacchaeus climbed (Luke 19:2) is not our sycamore but the mulberry-fig (*ficus sycomorus*), with leaves like mulberry leaves and fruit like figs (though, according to one commentator, insipid and woody in taste). The tree was carefully tended in Old Testament times; Amos the prophet of Tekoa was 'a dresser of sycamore trees' (Amos 7:14), and a certain Joash was the royal agent 'over the olive and sycamore trees of the Shephelah' (1 Chron. 27:28). These trees belonged to the lower regions of Palestine; Solomon made 'cedar as plentiful as the sycamore tree in the Shephelah' (1 Kings 10:27). Its wood was used for doors, boxes, and items of furniture. Tristram noted that 'there are still a few gnarled, aged sycomores among the ruins by the wayside at Jericho, and by the channels of the wadi Kelt'.

In New Testament times, if not earlier, Jericho was famous for its balm. Josephus calls it '*opobalsamum*, the most precious of all the local products' (*B.J.* 4.469). According to tradition, it was first brought to Judah by the Queen of Sheba on her visit to Solomon; 1 Kings 10:2 does not mention balm specifically, but it does say that she came 'with camels bearing spices'.

Balm is a gum that exudes from the plant *commifera opobalsamum*, originally from southern Arabia and Abyssinia. According to the geographer Strabo (born *c*. 64 B.C.),

> The balsam is of the shrub kind, resembling cytisus and terminthus [*medicago arborea* and *pistacia terebinthus*] and has a spicy flavour. The people make incisions in the bark and catch the juice in vessels. This juice is a glutinous milk-white substance; and when it is put up in small quantities, it solidifies; and it is remarkable for its cure of headache and incipient cataracts and of dimness of sight. Accordingly, it is costly; and also for the reason that it is produced nowhere else (*Geography*, XVI.41, Loeb translation).

Antony gave the balsam groves of Jericho to Cleopatra, from whom Herod the Great rented them until he regained possession of them. Both Pompey (63 BC) and Vespasian (AD 70) after their conquests of Judaea had balsam trees exhibited in Rome. Balm is also produced from an evergreen shrub (*balanites aegyptiaca*, 'false balm of Gilead'), which stands about 12–14ft. high and bears a purple fruit rather like an apple. The fruit is picked unripe, pounded, and boiled, and the oil then taken off. It grows in the plains by the Dead Sea; its Arabic name is *zukkum*.

The oasis of Jericho in ancient times produced a variety of food. The widest range of archaeological samples comes from the Early Bronze age (third millennium BC). Evidence from the Early Bronze tombs suggests that in addition to double-rowed barley (*hordeum distichum*), einkhorn (*triticum monococcum*), and emmer (*triticum dicoccum*), the diet included grapes, figs, horsebeans, lentils, chickpeas, onions, pomegranates, and dates. All of these could be grown locally. In medieval times sweetcane was introduced to the Jericho region and processed in the sugar mills whose ruins lie just west of Tell es-Sultan. Another important medieval crop was indigo, mentioned by the Arab geographer Idrisi in AD 1154. In modern times, the major crops are tomatoes, cucumbers, melons, citrus fruit and bananas, and the oasis of Jericho is a market garden.

Outside the oasis, the plain declines eastward toward the Jordan and becomes more barren and salty. Its vegetation is therefore mainly composed of halophytic shrubs. An edible plant of this salt plain is Jews' Mallow (*atriplex halimus*), or sea-purslane, perhaps the plant mentioned in Job 30:4 as eaten by men whom Job despises,

> they pick mallow and the leaves of bushes,
> and to warm themselves the roots of the broom.

The Hebrew name, *malluach*, is related to the word for salt and so suggests a salty plant. According to the Talmud, this plant served as food for Jews rebuilding the temple after the exile. Much less edible are the already mentioned wild gourd (*citrullus colocynthus*) and the so-called 'apple of Sodom' (*solanum sanctum* or *Sodomaeum*). This latter is an unpleasant plant, with thorny branches, and an inedible fruit, which looks rather like a tomato but when ripe contains only a few dry seeds. It is a symbol for Josephus of the disaster that struck Sodom,

> Still, too, one may see ashes reproduced in the fruits, which from their outward appearance would be thought edible, but on being plucked with the hand dissolve into smoke and ashes (*B.J.* 4.485, Loeb trans.).

Another plant which has been identified with the 'apple of Sodom' is the *calotropis procera* (Arabic ^c*osher*), a bush with glossy leaves observed in the region by the Swedish botanist Hasselqvist (AD 1751); Tristram a century later noted that it was extinct near Jericho, though found at Engedi further south along the Dead Sea coast. Better value is the hyssop, which Tristram identified with the caper (*capparis spinosa*) found in the Kedron valley and on the Mount of Temptation near Jericho; another variety (*capparis aegyptiaca*) grew plentifully on the Jericho plain. The flower buds of the caper can be pickled to produce a sauce. Others identify the hyssop with a marjoram (*origanum maru* or *aegyptiacum*) of the mint family. Another local plant is the camphire (*lawsonia inermis*), whose leaves can be pounded to produce the reddish-brown dye henna, used to stain the hands and feet. From a Jericho tomb came the remains of a wig, apparently dyed with henna. Along the bottom of the Wadi Qelt near Jericho grows the oleander bush, poisonous but spectacular with its pink flowers. This has been identified by some with the roses of Jericho mentioned in Ecclesiasticus 24:14, but the more usual identification is with the *anastatica hierochuntina*,

> a plant that looks like a dry withered ball when it is found lying on the fiercely hot sands of the barren plains surrounding the Dead Sea. It is also known as the resurrection flower and as the rose of Jericho because the dried up ball, blown about over large areas as a 'rolling thing' [cf. Isaiah 17:13, 'like a rolling thing before the whirlwind'], will at last come to a rest and, with the help of a little moisture, take root again (*All the Plants of the Bible*, p. 174).

Tristram explains it differently,

> The so-called *Rose of Jericho* has nothing to do with the scriptural allusions. It is a small ligneous cruciferous plant (*anastatica hierochuntina*), very inconspicuous, looking like some withered twig, which grows in the

TREE AT ELISHA'S FOUNTAIN.

Plate 3   *Zizyphus spina Christi* tree at Tristram's camp at Elisha's fountain.

sand in the hot barren plains round the Dead Sea. It derives its botanical name from its singular property of opening its minute flowers when plunged into water months after it has been gathered. . ... It is sought after as a relic by pilgrims (*The Natural History of the Bible*, p. 447).

If one moves from the plain down into the *zor*, instead of halophytic shrubs one meets trees. The tamarisk (*tamarix jordanis* and *tetragyna*) grows profusely, and charcoal from the Jericho tombs shows that it has been long established. Poplars flourish along the banks of the Jordan. The *acacia seyal*, the biblical Shittah tree (Isa. 41:18ff.), which produced the wood from which the ark was made (Exod. 25:10), is common in the wadi beds round the Dead Sea; on the other side of the Jordan from Jericho, in the plains of Moab, was Abel-shittim, 'the field of acacias' (Num. 33:49). Particularly common in the *zor* is the *zizyphus spina Christi* (Arabic *nubk*) (see Plate 3), which derives its Latin name from its presumed use on the head of Jesus at his passion, but whose main use is for hedges. Several Victorian travellers observed that the village and houses of Jericho were protected by this thorn. Another useful plant cultivated in this region in Old Testament times is flax (*linum usitatissimum*), stalks of which Rahab of Jericho laid on her roof to dry, later using them to conceal the Israelite spies. Isaiah 19:8 mentions it alongside cotton as an Egyptian plant. It was used for the manufacture of clothes; the fragments of textiles found in Jericho's Bronze age tombs are probably of vegetable origin, and may have been made of flax.

The plant life of the Jericho region is only one aspect of Jericho among several that underline the difference between Jericho and cities of the mountains and coastal plains of Palestine. Jericho is a place by itself, an oasis set in a hot, salty plain, hemmed in by semi-desert mountains to the west, and a river and another mountain chain to the east. Jericho lived in a world of her own, to some extent, with no other major settlement in sight to act as friend or enemy. Politically, Jericho lay and lies between the two focal points of Jerusalem and Amman, each just out of sight over the crest of the mountains west and east. Jericho was always a province apart, cut off from the centre of political life, and yet always an important physical link between those centres.

In the biblical period, at least, Jericho is mentioned rarely, and for the most part only when there is some movement from one side of the Jordan to the other – when the Israelites invade Palestine, when Ehud takes tribute to the king of Moab, when David sends ambassadors to the Ammonite king, when Elijah and Elisha cross the Jordan, or when the king of Judah tries to escape from the sack of Jerusalem. Jericho was the meeting point of the roads to the fords across the Jordan from ʿAin Feshka on the west coast of the Dead Sea, from Bethlehem, from Jerusalem, from Bethel, and from Shechem. On the east bank, roads come down to this point at the northern end of the Dead Sea from the biblical sites of Rabbath Ammon and Heshbon and the road that led south through Heshbon to Madeba and other Moabite cities. The Old Testament speaks of the fords of the Jordan; the *Survey of Western Palestine* noted five fords in the area, though not all of them were in use. The Madeba mosaic map pictures a ferry whose mast runs upstream of a rope stretched across the river to prevent the ferry being carried down on the fast stream. Today there are two bridges, the Allenby bridge east of Jericho and a second bridge further south, nearer the delta of the Jordan.

Jericho was inevitably a stopping point for travellers, such as David's luckless ambassadors (2 Sam. 10:5) or the third century BC official Zenon, who at Jericho dispensed 5 *artabai* of wheat among his travel party. Jericho was equally useful as a taxation centre, as the story of Zacchaeus makes clear: 'he was a chief tax-collector, and rich' (Luke 19:2). In the description of George Adam Smith,

Jericho is thus a city surrounded by resources. Yet in war she has always easily been taken. That her walls fell down at the sound of Joshua's trumpets is not exaggeration but the soberest summary of all her history. Judaea could never keep her. She fell to Northern Israel till Northern Israel perished. She fell to Bacchides and the Syrians. She fell to Aristobulus when he advanced on his brother Hyrcanus and Judaea. She fell without a blow to Pompey, and at the approach of Herod and again of Vespasian her people deserted her. It is also interesting to note that three invaders of Judaea – Bacchides, Pompey, and Vespasian – took Jericho before they attempted Jerusalem, although she did not lie upon their way to the latter, and that they fortified her, not, it is to be supposed, as a base of operations, so much as a source of supplies. This weakness of Jericho was due to two causes. An open pass came down on her from Northern Israel, and from this both part of her water supply could be cut off, and the hills behind her could be occupied. But besides this, her people seem never to have been distinguished for bravery; and, indeed, in that climate, how could they? Enervated by the great heat, which degrades all the inhabitants of the Ghor, and unable to endure on their bodies aught but linen, it was impossible that they could be warriors, or anything but irrigators, paddlers in water and soft earth. We forget how near neighbours they had been to Sodom and Gomorrah. No great man was born in Jericho; no heroic deed was ever done in her. She has been called 'the key' and 'the guardhouse' of Judaea; she was only the pantry. She never stood a siege, and her inhabitants were always running away (*The Historical Geography of the Holy Land*, pp. 182f.).

George Adam Smith's rhetoric is cruel; he judges the Jerichoans by the standards of a victorious empire. His knowledge of Jericho's history is limited, for he knew nothing of Neolithic and Bronze age Jericho, and of Jericho's pioneering place in the history of western man. He wrote when Jericho was 'but a few hovels and a tower on the edge of a swamp' (to quote his own description, which owes not a little to his predecessors), and he did not live to see the day when Jericho was once again a city of refugees, caught inevitably between two political centres. Jericho, however, an oasis in a wilderness, has resources which the more powerful cities around her do not have, and in a world short of food and energy she may well become once again a very desirable place to live. But the oasis has to be balanced against the wilderness, the perennial spring against the recurring earth tremors, the wealth against the defencelessness. This is the perpetual dilemma of Jericho's position.

For further reference

D. Baly, *The Geography of the Bible*, 2nd edn., Lutterworth Press, Guildford, 1974.

G. A. Smith, *The Historical Geography of the Holy Land*, Fontana Library edition, London, 1965.

G. Mountfort, *Portrait of a Desert*, Collins, London, 1965.

W. Walker, *All the Plants of the Bible*, Lutterworth Press, Guildford, 1958.

H. B. Tristram, *The Natural History of the Bible*, 9th edn, S.P.C.K., London, 1898.

2

Interpretation and excavation

Interest in ancient Jericho has never been purely academic. Jews and Christians alike have always had a deep-seated feeling for the land of the Bible, and to this day pilgrims and tourists follow well-trodden paths as they visit those biblical sites which have caught the imagination. From the fourth century AD onwards, many Christian pilgrims have left us records of their travels, and Jericho was one of the places they took care to visit. Its importance to the pilgrim was due to four biblical stories – Joshua's capture of Jericho (Josh. 6), Elisha's blessing of the spring (2 Kings 2:19–22), Hiel's refounding the city 'at the cost of' his first-born and youngest sons (1 Kings 16:34), and lastly the story of Jesus and Zacchaeus (Luke 19:1–10). Most travellers related what they saw at Jericho to details from these stories, and it is fascinating to read their accounts in chronological sequence to the present day and observe how the same features appear consistently, as if each traveller had carefully read his predecessors' accounts (as of course many had).

The first account comes from the 'pilgrim of Bordeaux', who travelled to Palestine in AD 333,

> On the right hand side, as one descends from the mount, behind a tomb, is the sycamore tree into which Zacchaeus climbed that he might see Christ. A mile-and-a-half from the town is the fountain of Elisha. Formerly if any woman drank of it she did not bear children. . . . Above the same fountain is the house of the harlot Rahab, to whom the spies came, and she hid them, and alone was saved when Jericho was destroyed. Here stood the city of Jericho, round whose walls the children of Israel circled with the Ark of the Covenant, and the walls fell down. Nothing is to be seen of it except the place where the Ark of the Covenant stood, and the twelve stones which the children of Israel brought out of the Jordan.

The house of Rahab, the spring of Elisha, Zacchaeus' tree all become standard features of later accounts. What is interesting in this account is that the Bordeaux pilgrim distinguishes between the Old Testament and the New Testament Jerichos, correctly locating the former with the tell above the spring and the latter with the village one and a half miles away. This distinction does not appear again so clearly until the nineteenth century. Thus in 700 Bishop Arculf noted that though three successive cities had been destroyed on the same site, the house of Rahab alone was left, but without a roof. Travellers coming to Jericho with the biblical stories in mind expected to find the remains of a large city, and their first comment was often one of surprise at the size and condition of the Jericho they saw. The Russian abbot Daniel (1106–7) described it as 'only a Saracen village'; similarly Sir John Maundeville began his account (1322) by noting that 'it is but a little village'. From the thirteenth century onwards another feature is regularly noted – a square tower. It is mentioned by Willibrand (1311), Redzivil (1614), Cotovicus (1619), and Henry Maundrell (1697), whose brief comment on Jericho is typical of many,

> at present only a poor nasty village of the Arabs. We were here carried to see a place where Zachaus' house is said to have stood – which is only an old square stone building, on the South side of Jericho (see Figure 3).

The Swedish botanist Hasselqvist, at Jericho in 1751, says almost exactly the same thing; in 1847 the squalid state of the tower, now occupied by a Turkish garrison, is described by W. R. Wilson and J. Wilson in their books. In 1862 an A. A. Isaacs tried to photograph the tower, but comments that 'It was no loss to us that our attempt proved unsuccessful'. Baedeker (1906) continues the tradition, noting that Jericho

> consists of a group of squalid hovels, the Serai (government building), and a few shops. . . . The only other curiosity in the village is a building on the S.E. side, resembling a tower. It probably dates from the Frank period. . . .

The tradition is up-dated by Jean Daniel-Rops (1955), who says of modern Jericho,

> It is commonplace town, with suburban villas and a golf club. The town which Jesus knew was higher up, on the site now occupied by the wretched hamlet of Er-riha.

From the mid-eighteenth century, however, there had been a scholarly interest in locating the precise sites of the Old Testament Jericho and the Herodian Jericho described by Josephus. In 1745 Richard Pococke described what appears to be the site now known to be the Hasmonaean and Herodian palaces to the west of Jericho. C. L. Irby and J. Mangles, travelling in 1818, say that they 'could trace no remains of the hippodrome which Josephus places here'. In 1821 J. S. Buckingham described the sites now identified as

Figure 3   The ruins of the medieval tower at Jericho.

the Hasmonaean and Herodian palaces and connected them with the Jericho of the first century AD. In 1841 Edward Robinson and Eli Smith looked at Tell es-Sultan with sharper eyes than their predecessors had:

> The mounds above the fountain are covered with substructures of unhewn stone; and others of the same kind are seen upon the plain towards the southwest. . . . Here then are traces enough of ancient foundations, such as they are; but none which could enable us to say definitely, This is the site of ancient Jericho. Around the fountain, where we should naturally look for its position, there is nothing which can well be referred to any large and important building; nothing, in short, which looks like the ruins of a great city, with a vast circus, perhaps, or other edifices.

Twenty-seven years later the mound was excavated by Capt. Charles Warren. East-west trenches were cut across Tell es-Sultan, with 8ft. square shafts downwards:

> Very little was found except pottery jars and stone mortars for grinding corn. The general impression given by the result of these excavations is that these mounds are formed by the gradual crumbling away of great towers or castles of sunburnt brick.

In fact, as became apparent in Kathleen Kenyon's excavations (1952–59), one of the shafts struck a wall which Kenyon identified as the Early Bronze town wall, and another missed the Neolithic stone tower by less than one metre. But Warren dug before the revolution in near eastern archaeology caused by Flinders Petrie's work on the importance of pottery and Mortimer Wheeler's refinement of the techniques of excavation, and though Warren reached Neolithic levels, he was unable to recognise them for what they were. Warren also excavated two mounds on the south bank of the Wadi Qelt, and one on the north bank. The first southern mound revealed an amphora, or large storage jar, with a Roman inscription, the second mound 'the remains of a masonry tower of no great pretensions'. Remains of a bridge over the wadi were found, and on the northern mound mud-brick walls and internal stone walls faced with coloured plaster.

These excavations were by modern standards of limited value, but they supported the belief, heralded by the work of Pococke, Buckingham, Robinson and Smith and finally expressed clearly in Condor and Kitchener's *Survey of Western Palestine* (1883), that Old Testament Jericho was to be found at Tell es-Sultan, New Testament Jericho at Tulul abu el-ᶜalaiq on the banks of the Wadi Qelt, and the Crusaders' Jericho at modern Eriha. This, as it has since turned out, is not quite correct, but at least the Wadi Qelt sites could with reason be associated with the Roman period. In 1875 Roman and Byzantine fragments were found in the village of Eriha, which showed that the village was much older than medieval.

In 1907–9 and 1911 Carl Watzinger and Ernst Sellin excavated on Tell es-Sultan and Tulul abu el-ᶜalaiq. They uncovered a large wall surrounding Tell es-Sultan on its northern, western and eastern sides, and on the tell itself a tower protected in front by a plastered earthen slope (often called a 'glacis') and associated with a double wall running north-south. Sellin and Watzinger held that an early third millennium BC settlement was destroyed at the end of the third or beginning of the second millennium, and that the subsequent city, protected by double walls above a sloping glacis, belonged to the first half of the second millennium BC and was destroyed by Joshua *c*. 1500 BC. A Canaanite settlement followed from the 15th–12th centuries BC. On the mound above the spring (in German the *Quellhügel*), on the southeast side of the tell, the excavators found houses which they ascribed to the period of the Israelite monarchy. They argued for the existence of Jericho from the 11th–8th century BC and attributed the large outer wall surrounding the tell to this period. They thought that the city was destroyed by the Assyrians in 721 and 701 BC, and by the Babylonians in 587 BC, and that a post-exilic settlement followed when the Jews returned from Babylon in 539 BC.

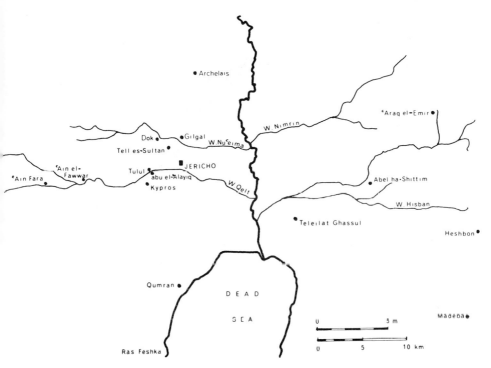

Figure 4   Map of the Jericho region, showing places mentioned in the text.

Some of Sellin and Watzinger's evidence for the Israelite Jericho of the monarchic and post-exilic periods has recently been re-examined, and found convincing. But their interpretation of the earlier walls and periods has been totally revised by the later work of Garstang and Kenyon. Sellin and Watzinger's final view that the large outer wall was later than the double wall on top of the mound turned out to be correct, though their dating was wrong. Sellin thought that the outer wall belonged to the ninth century BC and the double wall to the first half of the second millennium BC. Watzinger, however, later argued that the outer wall was destroyed c. 1600 BC, and that the double walls above it belonged to the third millennium BC, and that the Late Bronze age was not represented at all. In this he was essentially correct, but his solution was not popular with many who wished to date the double wall by reference to the capture of Jericho by Joshua in the second millennium BC.

In some ways Garstang's excavations of Tell es-Sultan (1930–36) were a step backward in the interpretation of the history of the tell. Garstang dated the outer retaining wall at the bottom of the slope to the Middle Bronze age (in agreement with Watzinger's later view), and the double wall above,

31

which showed signs of destruction by earthquake and fire, to the Late Bronze period. Below this supposed Late Bronze double wall, Garstang found a wall 10ft. thick which he attributed to the Early Bronze period. From the absence of 14th century BC Mycenaean pottery and Egyptian scarabs (seals made in the form of the Egyptian beetle *scarabaeus sacer*), Garstang dated the end of Late Bronze age Jericho to the turn of the 15th–14th century BC. Apart from one building (the 'Middle Building') which Garstang dated to the reign of Seti I (1309–1291 BC) and tentatively identified with the palace of Eglon of Moab (Judg. 3), and a successor on the same site, which Garstang suggested was a 12th century BC Philistine guardhouse, Garstang believed that Jericho lay in ruins until its restoration by Hiel in the 9th century BC (1 Kings 16:34). Garstang's work caused great excitement, and his dating of the destruction of Late Bronze Jericho featured in all subsequent attempts to date the Israelite exodus from Egypt and entry to the promised land. If Garstang was right, the Exodus must belong to the 15th century, and the incoming Israelites might be related to or identified with the Habiru of the Amarna letters of the first half of the 14th century BC, in which kings of Palestinian towns complain to Pharaoh that they are suffering from the military activities of the Habiru and others. A major defect of this dating, however, was that it left unexplained the biblical reference (Exod. 1:13) to the oppressed Israelites' part in the building of the store cities of Rameses II (1294–1224 BC).

Garstang's work, however, broke new ground in its recognition of the Mesolithic and Neolithic stages of Jericho's existence. Garstang ascribed the beginnings of the Mesolithic town to *c.* 4000 BC, when the inhabitants used microliths (i.e. very small flint implements) and lived, perhaps, in rock shelters. The first Neolithic period was marked by houses with burnished plaster floors and walls, periodically rebuilt as damp and earth movements caused decay. To the second Neolithic period Garstang ascribed a temple with portico, antechamber and inner chamber, and votive figurines of clay, domestic implements such as mortars, flint tools and arrowheads, and the beginnings of pottery, which Garstang dated to *c.* 3400 BC (Figure 5). Particularly interesting in view of Kenyon's later discoveries are the two groups of heads modelled in clay described below. Garstang's dating of the Neolithic period to the fourth millennium BC, however, led to his belief that Jericho was isolated from the rest of the ancient near east at this time, for by this period Egypt and Babylonia were much more advanced than Jericho appeared to be.

Garstang's work, therefore, introduced a new dimension to the study of ancient Jericho, but it also introduced new problems. The problem of the date of the Exodus continued to vex historians of Israel, and many scholars,

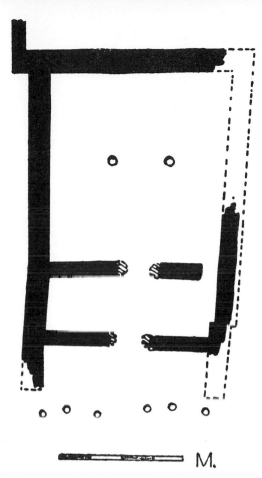

Figure 5   Plan of 'stone age shrine' excavated by J. Garstang.

dissatisfied with Garstang's dating, attempted to redate the destruction of Jericho. W. F. Albright suggested 1375–1300 BC, L. H. Vincent argued for c. 1250 BC. In 1951 Kathleen Kenyon published a careful study (undertaken at the invitation of Garstang himself) of Garstang's interpretation of the stratigraphy of Tell es-Sultan. Kenyon's article confirmed that the glacis and surrounding wall belonged to Middle Bronze II (thus agreeing with both Garstang and Watzinger), but demonstrated that the layer beneath it belonged to Early Bronze III (c. 2600–2400 BC) by a comparison of its pottery with that from Garstang's tomb A4. (This demonstration paved the way for a later redating of the 'double wall' on the crest of the mound, these two walls being found to belong to different strata from the Early Bronze age.) From a re-examination of the buildings on the *Quellhügel* Kenyon showed that there was evidence of continuous occupation in this area from Early Bronze III through the Intermediate Early Bronze–Middle Bronze period to the Middle Bronze age, that the pottery of the final period was contemporary with the pottery from strata E and D at Tell Beit Mirsim and strata XI–X at Megiddo, and that therefore the destruction of these buildings should be dated to the sixteenth century BC, *c.* 1560 BC. Kenyon argued that the area was subsequently unoccupied for some 150 years.

This led to a major difference between Garstang's conclusions and Kenyon's. As we have seen, Garstang believed that Tell es-Sultan was occupied in the 15th century and destroyed *c.* 1400 BC, thereafter remaining largely ruined for several centuries. Kenyon argued, on the basis of improved knowledge of the sequence of Late Bronze age pottery since Garstang's excavations, that pottery typical of Late Bronze I (*c.* 1500–1400 BC) was completely missing from the tell and from the tombs excavated by Garstang. There was no evidence of a 15th century city and no evidence of walls destroyed by earthquake and fire at the end of that century. There was, however, (again contrary to Garstang's view) evidence of some slight occupation at Tell es-Sultan in the 14th century BC.

Kenyon's analysis of Garstang's work was vindicated by her own excavations on Tell es-Sultan (1952–59). For biblical scholars, the most interesting part of Kenyon's work was that relating to the existence and dating of Late Bronze age Jericho. Some scholars wished to date the exodus from Egypt and the Israelite capture of Jericho in the 15th century BC, others in the 13th century. Garstang's conclusions had suited the former group, but Kenyon's findings suited neither. Kenyon's work has shown that there is no archaeological evidence for the existence of a city at Tell es-Sultan in either the 15th or the 13th–12th centuries BC. It has also become clear that these gaps cannot be explained by the theory that the Late Bronze age evidence has been eroded away by wind and rain, for such erosion leaves traces in the wash at the foot of the mound, and no such traces have been discovered for the Late Bronze period at the foot of Tell es-Sultan (Figure 6).

Of much greater interest in many quarters has been Kenyon's demonstration that the history of Tell es-Sultan goes back as early as the eighth, ninth or even tenth millennium BC (Garstang dated his earliest findings to the fourth millennium). Kenyon's work has raised a large debate about the date of the origin and development of urban civilisation and of the beginnings of settlement in the ancient Near East. This debate arose largely because on Kenyon's evidence the beginnings of agriculture, the domestication of animals, and the organisation of people into the structure of a walled settlement at Tell es-Sultan appeared to predate similar phenomena elsewhere in the Near East by several millennia. On the other hand, Kenyon's demon-

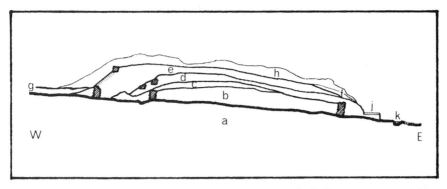

Figure 6   A section through Tell es-Sultan: *a*. bedrock; *b*. Pre-pottery Neolithic; *c*. Pottery Neolithic; *d*. Early Bronze; *e*. Middle Bronze; *f*. Late Bronze; *g*. Iron; *h*. later deposits; *j*. road; *k*. spring.

stration of Pre-pottery Neolithic B, Pre-pottery Neolithic A, and 'proto-Neolithic' settlements at Tell es-Sultan has helped fill in the previously existing historical gap between the Natufian peoples and Neolithic peoples of Palestine.

Meanwhile, other sites in the Jericho region have been re-explored and excavated. In 1950 J. Kelso and D. C. Baramki began work at Tulul abu el-ᶜalaiq, first excavated by Warren. The excavators thought that the tells concealed the two towers, Threx and Taurus, captured by Pompey in 63 BC, and that the subsequent Herodian development of the site marked the civic centre of New Testament Jericho. J. B. Pritchard excavated a large building on the south side of the wadi which he identified as a gymnasium. Subsequent exploration of this complex of ruins by E. Netzer, however, has shown that this is not the site of New Testament Jericho. The northern mound or tell was originally a Hasmonaean palace, later covered by an artificial mound; beside it was a swimming pool. The 'gymnasium' was Herod the Great's first palace, later incorporated into the grander palace buildings and gardens built along each bank of the wadi. The southern mound also belonged to this later period, and contained a bath-house (see Figures 25, 26).

These discoveries reopened the question of the site of New Testament Jericho. Evidence for a post-exilic Jericho had been found at Tell es-Sultan, but there was no indication of later occupation there. A hoard of Seleucid coins discovered on the northern edge of the modern Jericho (the latest coin being dated 103/2 BC) may support the possibility that New Testament Jericho lay where modern Jericho lies, but more definite evidence is needed.

It is now almost a century since the first excavations took place at Jericho.

But not even a century of excavation has been enough to answer all the questions raised by this site. Excavation has created new problems for the historian, and there is no reason to doubt that, economic circumstances permitting, excavation at Jericho will continue into the future. Kathleen Kenyon has remarked that there has been renewed archaeological activity at Jericho approximately every twenty-five years since Condor and Kitchener's time. Perhaps we may look forward to the next major excavation there in the early years of the next millennium.

For further reference

J. Wilkinson, *Jerusalem Pilgrims before the Crusades*, Aris and Phillips, Warminster, 1978.

C. R. Condor and H. H. Kitchener, *The Survey of Western Palestine*, III, Committee of the Palestine Exploration Fund, London, 1883.

E. Sellin and C. Watzinger, *Jericho: Die Ergebnisse der Ausgräbungen*, Leipzig, 1913.

J. Garstang and J. B. E. Garstang, *The Story of Jericho*, 2nd ed., Marshall, Morgan and Scott, London, 1948.

K. M. Kenyon, *Digging up Jericho*, Benn, London, 1957.

J. Kelso and D. C. Baramki, *Excavations at New Testament Jericho and Khirbet en-Nitla*, *Annual of the American Schools of Oriental Research*, 29–30 (1949–1951), New Haven, 1955.

E. Netzer, G. Foerster-Gabriella Bacchi, *sub* 'Jericho' in M. Avi-Yonah (Ed.), *Encyclopedia of Archaeological Excavations in the Holy Land*, Oxford, 1976, vol. 2, pp. 564–575.

3

The beginnings of city life

It is not easy to begin a history of what has been called 'the oldest city of the world'. The earliest recognisable building on the site has recently been given a radio-carbon dating of *c*. 9250, which takes the beginnings of Jericho back into the tenth millennium BC. But we cannot simply recount the history of Jericho from that date as if it were a sequence of local events unrelated to the surrounding world. Jericho, though at the bottom of a hot and enervating valley, near a river which provided a certain obstacle to movement, did not exist as a 'lost city', sealed off from contact with surrounding societies. A review of her career, however, suggests that she prospered most when the surrounding territories were without strong, centralised political institutions, and consisted of small, independent towns or villages. When the centralised states of Israel, Judah, Ammon and Moab emerged in the biblical period, Jericho became a relatively unimportant place. The context in which Jericho existed is an important part of her history.

In the tenth millennium BC Palestine was beginning to emerge from the Palaeolithic age and enjoyed a culture known today as 'Kebaran' after a site near Mount Carmel where the typical features of the period were first found. The people lived in caves or on camp-sites, herding goats and gazelles, and preparing with their pestles and mortars wild grain cut by their flint sickles. They worked animal bones for needles, shells for decorations, and flints for tools (Figure 7). Succeeding this society, and not unlike it, was the Natufian society, named after a site found in 1928 about 30 kms north-west of Jerusalem. This period marks the change to the Mesolithic age in Palestine, and from it comes the first evidence of occupation on the site of Tell es-Sultan. It was a time of increasing warmth in Palestine, and as the ice retreated higher up the slopes of the mountains round the Fertile Crescent, the Jordan valley became drier. Perhaps the level of the Dead Sea fell slightly. The Natufians moved away from the coastal sites favoured by the Kebaran people, but in many respects they continued the Kebaran way of life. They lived in caves or on open-air sites in circular dwellings built on stone bases of 7–9 metres diameter, probably roofed by reeds on a wooden frame, the floor sunk a little below ground level. Stone mortars, saddle querns

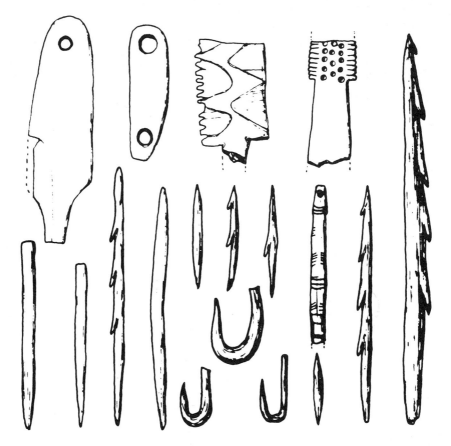

Figure 7   Natufian objects from Kebara (after Turville-Petre).

and storage pits, and sickles whose flint blades were held into a grooved
bone haft by bitumen or vegetable resins suggest the preparation and storage of cereals. The bones of goat, gazelle, boar, with heavy axes and scrapers,
and lunate (i.e., crescent shaped) flint microliths used for barbs in arrows or
spears, reveal herding and hunting activity; harpoons, fish-hooks and net-
weights found at Eynan near Lake Huleh indicate fishing. A bone-sickle
haft carved to the form of a deer, a gazelle carved from limestone, and the
stone carving of an embracing couple show artistic interest and ability.
Particularly interesting in view of discoveries from Jericho are the Natufian
burial practices. Bodies were usually buried in groups, in a contracted
position below the hut floor or cave terrace. Sometimes a number of skulls
seem to have been detached from their bodies before the flesh had totally
decayed, and buried together in pits. Heads were sometimes decorated with

Plate 4   The Lower Natufian period sanctuary at Tell es-Sultan.

dentalia shells, and skeletons with shells or paint, and necklaces or anklets made of gazelle teeth or bones. In some places the burial pit was covered by stone paving; in some cases, the burials are secondary, i.e., the bones were buried, and then later gathered and reburied in a final resting place.

It was to this world that the first known inhabitants of Jericho belonged. On the bedrock in site E towards the northern end of the tell, Kenyon found an area of clay 3.5 × 6.5 metres left on the otherwise cleared bedrock. A wall had been built round it, with wooden posts set in at intervals. The wall also contained two large stone blocks with holes bored through to receive posts. Kenyon suggested that these would have been totem poles or something similar, the area being a sanctuary which Kenyon dated by a lunate and a bone harpoon head to the Lower Natufian period (Plate 4). Sickle blades, borers and scrapers were also found, and old mortars were used as building material; the Natufian Jerichoans like their contemporaries harvested grain and scraped animal skins. Jericho lay in the range of distribution of wild barley (*hordeum spontaneum*), and the wild ancestor of emmer wheat (*triticum dicoccoides*). Their descendants, two-rowed barley (*hordeum distichum*) and emmer (*triticum dicoccum*), together with einkhorn (*triticum boeoticum*), are evidenced at Tell es-Sultan from Pre-pottery Neolithic onwards, and the beginnings of grain farming clearly began earlier.

There is some evidence that towards the end of the Natufian period some Palestinian sites were deserted for a time. But occupation at Jericho may have been continuous in view of its perennial spring, and there is evidence in site M just west of the centre of the present mound of a lengthy occupation in what Kenyon calls a 'proto-Neolithic' period. There is a 4 metre thick deposit of what was probably a succession of clay floors and mud walls. The humps visible in the section of the excavation are perhaps all that is left of the bases of these walls, which were constructed above of skin and branches and below of cricket ball sized lumps of clay. This succession of mud buildings created the nucleus of what was to become Tell es-Sultan, and it presumably started on ground just above the outlet of the spring. If this was a seasonal camp, it was regularly used over quite a long period, and is perhaps evidence that the nomadic people who used to visit the earlier sanctuary near the spring were now beginning to settle into a more permanent home.

Jericho's potential as a food-producing region was doubtless responsible for the enormous expansion of the site which took place at the end of the ninth millennium BC. The 'proto-Neolithic' camp developed into a walled town of over ten acres, the hunting community became a farming community and perhaps also a trading community. This is the period known, since Kenyon's work, as Pre-pottery Neolithic A (PPNA). It developed without

40

Plate 5   A Pre-pottery Neolithic A house at Tell es-Sultan.

any apparent break from the proto-Neolithic stage. The Jerichoans of this PPNA period are the same people as the earlier Natufians, using much the same flint and bone tools, with sickle blades, a few arrows and other microliths, though adding the larger picks (for agricultural work) and chisels, axes and adzes (for working timber). They had round houses, probably developed from the mud-walled huts of proto-Neolithic. They continued to hunt and perhaps to herd gazelle, which supplied the major part of their meat, and also cattle, goat, and boar. There is still no clear evidence of domestic animals. But the important new feature which probably did more than anything else to create the new thriving community of PPNA Jericho was the domestication of cereals, notably the two-rowed barley and emmer wheat. Fig pips, and evidence of leguminous plants were also found. Kenyon noted that the collection of wild grain and the hunting of wild animals alone were insufficient to feed a town as large as PPNA Jericho, and that some way of producing food was necessary; the key to this lay in using the spring for irrigation.

It is worth pausing a moment to consider the food-producing potential of Jericho. In modern times this region is an important food-producing area, and this was probably the case in ancient times. Jericho had a number of features rarely found together elsewhere in Palestine. It was built on alluvial soil washed down from the Judaean mountains to the west and spreading downhill to the Jordan valley. It had a spring with a steady perennial flow based on the reservoir of water which drained to harder levels through the soft surface rock of the Judaean hills, and so down to emerge at their foot. Having emerged, the water spread out over flat ground which sloped gently towards the Jordan, and so watered a fairly large area. The surrounding country had variety – deep wadis cut into the hills to the west, hill grazing country, woods and forest near the river, and open bushland. This was an area where wild animals had cover, food and water, and where vegetation had every chance of survival through hot summers. Animals could be caught at the spring, crops (when the technique was learned) could be harvested two or even three times a year. Peter Dorrell (in *Archaeology and the Levant*, ed. P. R. Moorey and P. J. Parr, London, 1978, pp. 11–18) has made some interesting calculations about the feeding of Jericho's citizens, starting from the known size of PPNA Jericho (ten acres). He argues that the area would allow about 660 dwellings and a population of about 3000–3500, which would consume roughly 2500 goats, 1700 gazelles, 1300 oxen, 1400 pigs, and about 440 tons of cereal, fruit and vegetables a year (assuming meat and cereals are eaten in roughly equal proportion). This would involve catching up to 19 animals a day and farming about 440 hectares (at two crops per annum) or 290 hectares (three crops), and less for a smaller population. The

Plate 6   The Neolithic tower.

Jericho oasis today covers 980 hectares (with more sophisticated irrigation, but with a much greater domestic use of water). That is to say that the Jericho region could easily support a settled population of two or three thousand people. Dorrell also argues that 'no qualitative or quantitative change in the economic way of life or the social structure of the community is demanded by the minor innovations needed to develop a food producing community after a hunting or collecting economy. The line between the two economies is not so definite as was once thought.'

Clearly, the feeding of a population on this scale demands some social organisation, and it is the presence of this that is so well demonstrated by the archaeological evidence from PPNA Jericho. The earliest levels show round or oval buildings whose floor is sunk about half a metre below ground level (Plate 5). They are entered by a short porch; steps, originally with wooden treads, led down to floor level. The walls were made of 'hog-back' mud bricks, oval in shape, with a flat base and curved top. The roofing was perhaps clay or skins on a frame of branches, but, according to the excavator, the amount of brick in the debris of the collapse suggests that the roofs were domed. These houses were found in sites E, M, and D at Tell es-Sultan, and the fact that they were found beneath the earliest stone walls of Jericho suggests that this early PPNA community was quite large, spreading on its western side, at least, beyond the line of the later wall. It seems that this expanding community came to need a defence system, possibly because Jericho, as a prosperous area, was attracting too many immigrants from poorer areas, or raiding nomads, or both. The line of settlement was brought back on the western side, and a stone wall 1.5 metres wide was built. The excavated portion was preserved to a height of 5.75 metres. Just behind it was built a solid tower, 8.5 metres in diameter, surviving to a height of 7.75 metres, with a doorway on the eastern side at the bottom, and an internal staircase to the roof of which 22 steps remain intact (Plate 6). The tower was perhaps basically a watch-tower rather than a bastion, for it is not built into the wall but lies inside it. This fact makes it unlikely that there were other towers, as has sometimes been suggested. It may have been built on what was then the highest point of the nucleus tell in order to command the widest view.

In a second phase, the settlement's wall was rebuilt 3.5 metres west of the original wall, and a ditch was cut out of the bedrock in front of it 9.5 metres wide and 2.25 metres deep. What appear to be storage rooms or tanks (one contained some remains of charred grain, others had sedimentary deposits and a water channel) were built round the base of the tower, blocking the staircase entrance, which could now be entered only through a trapdoor. When these tanks became silted up and disused, a skin wall 1 metre thick was built above them round the original tower, now totally blocking the staircase entrance. The town wall was raised in height, and a new set of storage rooms built above the old ones round the tower. Clearly the ground level within the walls was steadily rising through this period as buildings decayed and were replaced, and altogether some twenty-five building levels of PPNA Jericho were excavated, covering perhaps a millennium. Each level therefore perhaps represents about 40 years or two generations. The area covered was about ten acres; the original wall, first discovered in Trench I on the middle of the western side of the tell and later found surviving to a height of 2.1 metres in Trench III at the south end and to one course at the north end, was perhaps about 700 yards long altogether. The wall of the later phases of PPNA does not appear in the northern and southern trenches. It probably lay a little beyond the outer ends of these trenches, concealed by the later Middle Bronze wall. Thus PPNA Jericho at its north and south ends reached the very limits of the modern tell. Exactly how far it extended on the east side cannot be determined, as the area has been eroded by the wadi and the modern road. Dorrell calculates that the construction of the original wall would have required about 12000 metric tons of limestone (collected rather than quarried, unless the rock-cut ditch was used as a quarry), and would have involved 200 men for one week. This seems a very short time indeed, unless the labour force was very well organised.

It has been suggested that the reason for such strong defences was not only the general desirability of Jericho as a place to live comfortably, but also the wealth that Jericho acquired from trade. Anati argued that the development of agriculture was not enough to explain the unparalleled growth of Jericho. Other sites could offer the right conditions for growing cereals and hunting animals, but they did not expand like Jericho. Conversely, if Jericho's agriculture was so productive, why were there long periods when Jericho was apparently abandoned? Anati argued therefore that Jericho became rich by trading the natural resources of the region – salt, bitumen, and sulphur, all of which could be found in and around the Dead Sea. In return Jericho received obsidian from Turkey, turquoise from Sinai, and cowrie shells from the Mediterranean coast. In what sense these commodities created wealth is not clear. They must have been the luxuries that came as extras to add to the colour of life. How far their presence in Jericho was the result of organised trade and a professional merchant class we do not know, but certainly there must have been a fair amount of contact between Jericho and the outside world, at least between Jericho and other Palestinian sites, as is shown by the similarity of implements and tools through the region.

It is clear that PPNA Jericho, though a development of the earlier 'proto-Neolithic' settlement with its clay floors and huts, has in developing become something of a different order altogether. For a thousand years or more a slight mound of ten acres was occupied by people who produced about twenty-five occupation levels, four phases of city wall, organised the food supply for up to 3000 people, and perhaps entered upon limited trading relationships and other contacts with outsiders. A much debated question is whether this enables us to speak of the existence of a 'city' and of 'civilisation' in the eighth millennium BC. Everything depends, of course, on one's definition of those terms; when they were first used, it was argued that the excavated evidence may point to a large, organised community, but for a 'city' something more is required – in particular, evidence of a society which depends upon the co-ordination of a number of specialist activities outside the range of food production, including workmen with various skills, tradesmen, and administrators. Clearly it is unfair to call Jericho a 'city' and then judge it by reference to the modern city, but equally clearly this large, walled community represented an important advance on the previous stage of occupation of the site.

However, what made the description of Jericho as a city really difficult when it was first proposed was that Jericho was being dated much earlier than was expected for such a Neolithic site. Garstang had dated Neolithic Jericho to the fourth millennium BC. More recently, Jarmo, in north-eastern Iraq, with its pre-pottery Neolithic strata, incipient agriculture and domestication of animals, had been dated c. 4750 BC. Kenyon, however, was dating the early town wall at Jericho c. 7800 BC, and the end of PPNA to c. 6779. More recently, the dates for both Jarmo and Jericho have been raised; the excavator of Jarmo now thinks that Jarmo existed for a period of about 250 years c. 6750, and the latest radio-carbon dates for the beginning and end of the PPNA period at Jericho are 8340 ± 200 − 6935 ± 155 BC.

Jericho remains the earliest known example of a walled and defended settlement, but there were other contemporary settlements in Palestine and Syria and further abroad – e.g., Wadi Fallah (Nahal Oren) near Mount Carmel in Palestine, and Mureybet south east of Aleppo in Syria – showing much the same cultural traits. Mureybet III was probably contemporary with the later stages of PPNA Jericho, and in this level alongside the round houses were found rectangular houses with paved and plastered floors and plastered walls, features which did not occur at Jericho until Pre-pottery Neolithic B in the seventh millennium BC. At El Khiam, only twenty miles from Jericho, there was a small open site on the terraces of a wadi. It was apparently not sedentary, concentrating on hunting rather than on agriculture, and it did not develop in the same way that Jericho did. Clearly there could be regional differences within the one culture. What could happen in a barren wadi valley and what could happen in a fertile plain like Jericho's were two very different things.

The PPNA settlement at Tell es-Sultan lasted until somewhere between 7350 and 7000 BC, after which the tell appears to have been abandoned for a time. On the west side the town wall collapsed, and the upper levels of the houses built up against its inside and the upper courses of the old tower were eroded away, the debris filling the ditch outside the wall. Why the PPNA settlement came to an end is not known; earthquake, pestilence, invasion, or decline in the fertility of the local soil through overworking have all been suggested. In view of the period of abandonment that followed until c. 7000 BC or soon after, this last is perhaps the most likely cause.

The most noticeable thing about the Pre-pottery Neolithic B culture (PPNB) which follows is that many more PPNB than PPNA sites are known, particularly in Syria and Lebanon. The second noticeable feature is that towards the end of the period pottery is beginning to appear, in the form of a dark burnished ware first found in northern Iraq and later on the Levant coast (though not yet as far south as Jericho). Among the southern PPNB sites, such as Wadi Fallah on the coast, and Beidha near Petra in Jordan, Jericho was much the largest. This is again probably to be explained by favourable conditions there for agriculture, hunting, herding, and rearing animals. But Jericho is clearly part of a cultural milieu recognisable virtually throughout Syria and Palestine.

Settlement in this period has moved away from caves and their terraces to the sites which are to become tells. The houses become rectangular in shape, their floors carefully plastered and sometimes coloured, the plaster often curving from floor to wall and covering the wall to waist height. The flint industry changes; there are proportionately fewer arrowheads (though they have a better tang than previously), and more longer blades, sometimes with denticulated edges and made to be set into a sickle-haft or some other handle. The heavier agricultural tools – axes, adzes, picks – and the microliths both disappear; digging sticks (pointed sticks set through a holed stone added to give weight) are used for breaking up the earth, and denticulated flint blades for cutting wood. Querns become more elongated and rectangular, being open at one end and having a flat rim round the other three sides. Crop-growing has become an established feature of the economy; peas, lentils, chickpeas, and vetch appear in addition to the cereals known in PPNA. The grain-size of two-row barley has increased considerably in PPNB. At other sites of this period pistachio nuts were also eaten.

With the development of food production went the domestication of useful animals. From a study of the horn-cores of goats found in the PPNB levels of Jericho, F. E. Zeuner (*Palestine Exploration Quarterly* (1955), pp. 70–86) argued that since these cores differed profoundly from those of the only native wild goat left in modern times (Sinaitic ibex), and compared closely with those of the domesticated screw-horned goats of the Bronze age, the goats at PPNB Jericho were domesticated. It was in this period that the gazelle ceased to be the main source of meat at Jericho and was replaced by the goat. The domestication of sheep, too, may belong to this period, the size of the animal (to judge from sheep bones discovered) having decreased slightly since the PPNA period. Whether the dog was domesticated by this stage is debated. The evidence is slender, very few bones being found on the tell, probably because dogs were not eaten as food and their carcases were thrown out of the city. An isolated cat tooth was found in the earliest but one level of PPNB Jericho. The specimen was small, and Zeuner (*Palestine Exploration Quarterly* (1958), pp. 52–55) suggests that cats had established themselves long enough to have become smaller than their cousins in the wild (which in turn suggests that a settlement which accepted cats had been established for some time). The domestication of cats surely goes hand in hand with the establishment of human settlements, for cats eat the rats and mice which feed on the food stored or wasted by men. Men continued to hunt in PPNB; at Munhata near the Sea of Galilee gazelle bones made up 44% of the total which included pig, goat and aurochs bones; at Beisamun, however, aurochs bones were more common. There is no evidence that men ate fish, snails, freshwater mussels or birds (as they had done earlier at some places), or that they tried to domesticate large animals such as cattle. Presumably the smaller goats were easier to handle, and produced only as much meat as could be cooked and eaten at the time of slaughter; there was no refrigeration for storage in PPNB Jericho.

How the people of the PPNA and PPNB cultures were related is not clear. The usual view is that the PPNB people were quite different from their predecessors; Kenyon suggested that the walls of PPNA Jericho had been built to defend it from the PPNB people. But it is unlikely that these peoples were totally unrelated. Some features of PPNA have survived into PPNB without much change, and at Beidha, near Petra, contemporary with Jericho's PPNB, there is a sequence of occupation levels which shows development from the round hut to the round house typical of PPNA Jericho, and then to a polygonal phase which makes the transition to the rectangular structures typical of PPNB Jericho, a phase destroyed by fire at Beidha *c.* 6650 BC (Plate 7). Probably Beidha was influenced by new PPNB elements arriving from the Syrian region in the course of the seventh millennium BC. It may be a mistake to emphasise too heavily the differences between PPNA and PPNB and so exaggerate the discontinuity between them at Jericho, particularly when the length of the time gap between them is so uncertain.

Plate 7   A Pre-pottery Neolithic B house at Tell es-Sultan.

The PPNB settlement at Jericho covered much the same area as its predecessor. In its first stages it was apparently undefended (as PPNA Jericho had been at the same stage), the houses spreading to the west over the ruins of the PPNA wall. The houses were built of hand-made bricks, 'in shape rather like a flattened cigar, with the surface impressed with a herringbone pattern by pairs of prints of the brickmaker's thumb' (Kenyon). This impressed pattern gave a key for the mortar, probably made of mud or lime. No complete houseplan was found, but enough was found to show that the houses consisted of a central courtyard with rooms either side. The rooms were rectangular, with slightly rounded corners, and quite large, even by modern standards; Kenyon notes the measurements of two examples as 6.5 × 4 metres, and 7 × 3 metres. Smaller rooms off them were perhaps for storage, access being through an opening in the wall. Storage bins were also placed in this courtyards. One courtyard was traced through fourteen successive building stages; its boundary moved slightly eastwards as time passed, but it retained its length of 6.5 metres. As is shown by the central hearths and layers of ashes, the courtyard was the place for cooking. Inside, the rooms had clay floors with a surface of lime plaster, coloured red, orange, pink, or plain white, and given a polished finish by a burnishing process. Rush mats were used to cover the floors (the remnants of one showed where an ant had eaten a track across it), and the remains of four round mats, compared with one rectangular mat, suggested that the tradition of round mats survived in PPNB from the round huts of PPNA. These PPNB houses seem to have continued unchanged in shape through something like twenty-five rebuildings (which may represent a period of about a thousand years).

Two rooms at Jericho may have been designed for religious purposes. In one case, a house room had been divided off, and a niche was built. Inside was set a stone which appeared to serve as the pedestal for another stone found nearby in the debris of the building. This stone was a piece of volcanic rock, 46 cms high and 18 cms wide, originally brought from a district about 8 miles the other side of the Jordan. In the Jericho building, it may have served as a cult object. In another rectangular room, 6 × 4 metres, was a central basin. The plaster about it was scorched. At each end of the room were rounded and perhaps originally domed annexes. The arrangement suggests ceremonial purposes, but there is no other evidence to suggest what they were. Two small female figurines were found in PPNB Jericho. One is badly preserved; the other has lost her head, but in her stance, with her hands supporting her breasts, she is typical of later figurines usually interpreted as representing the goddess of fertility. Female figurines were also found at other PPNB sites. The animal figurines of goat and ibex at Beidha, or of horned animals at Jericho and Munhata, may have magical or religious

Plate 8   A Pre-pottery Neolithic B plastered skull.

significance, unless, as has sometimes been suggested, they were made as children's toys. But whatever their purpose, they show an appreciation of the uses to which clay can be put.

Perhaps the most striking feature of PPNB Jericho, and certainly the best known, is the practice of plastering skulls (Plate 8). A small piece of bone carved in the form of a human face, apparently designed to be sewn on to something, showed interest in the human head which was underlined by the discovery of a number of skulls. The first to be found was that of an elderly man buried in the corner of a room beneath the floor. A group of seven skulls was then discovered on the edge of site DI, again beneath the plastered floor of a house; later, two more were discovered ten feet away beneath the same floor, and yet one more in a different part of the tell. But the group of seven was in a tumbled heap in the debris of the collapse or destruction of the house which preceded the plaster floor. This means that the plastered skulls did not belong to the period of the plaster floor beneath which they lay, but to the period of the preceding house. They were apparently preserved and perhaps venerated in this house, beneath whose floor were found some forty skeletons, buried without skulls in some disorder. The skulls seem to have been removed from these bodies after their burial and before decomposition was complete – a somewhat gruesome business. Further excavation revealed that it had been regular practice in the PPNB period at Jericho to bury the body beneath the floor of the house, removing the skull.

Evidence of similar practice has since been discovered at other contemporary sites – Sheikh Ali south of the Sea of Galilee, Tell Ramad near Damascus, Beidha near Petra, and pre-pottery Hacilar and Çatal Hüyük in Turkey. But what made these Jericho skulls so interesting is the way they had been treated. The head was filled with clay, and external features – nose, mouth, ears, eyebrows, cheeks, jawline (for the lower jawbone was not used except in one case) – were moulded on to the skull with plaster. Paint was used to convey colouring, and in one case to show hair and a headdress, and in another a moustache. Pieces of shell were placed, with a slight gap between them, in the eye sockets; in one case a cowrie shell was used.

Since the Jericho discoveries a similar group of plastered skulls has been found at Tell Ramad; these too used plaster, paint, and bivalve or cowrie shells. Here the skulls appear to have been supported by 25 cms high headless seated clay figures. Clearly these skulls were meant to be seen; they were in fact exhibited. The purpose of the exhibiting is not clear, but it was probably to demonstrate the continuity between the previous and the present generations. Kenyon suggested that the men of the PPNB culture believed that by preserving the skulls of their predecessors they were preserving for their own generation the wisdom of their ancestors. If so, these people were

Plate 9   A painted plaster head from Tell es-Sultan, excavated by J. Garstang. -

making a connection between heads and wisdom not always made in antiquity. The practice seems to have developed into something more formal and less grisly; in what were probably late PPNB levels, John Garstang found in 1935 what had been perhaps two groups of three heads, each group perhaps representing a male, a female, and a child. The heads were flat, two-dimensional objects almost life-size, made of unbaked, moulded clay (Plate 9). Shells were used for eyes, and paint for the hair and the beard. The head breaks off at the neck; how much was modelled below the neck is not clear. Also found were models of a very stylised torso and head, the head being little more than a roughly rectangularly shaped flat piece above the torso, with some features rather crudely painted on. These latter have nothing like the elegance of the plastered skulls or even of the plaques. The purpose of these objects remains uncertain. They may have represented gods or ancestors.

The PPNB period seems to have lasted for at least a millenium at Jericho, and radio-carbon dates give the extreme ranges as $7379 \pm 102 - 5845 \pm 160$ BC. It seems best to suppose that the period roughly coincided with the seventh millenium BC. In Trench I, 26 building stages were traced (only 19 in squares E II, III, where Garstang's excavations had probably removed several layers of PPNB). Houses of the period were in fact found all over the tell, covering at least eight acres. At its highest point, the tell now reached 24ft. above the level of the surrounding plain. The earlier PPNB settlement existed without benefit of a defensive wall, for the first PPNB wall (from the evidence in Trench I and site M) was built by cutting foundations into the first PPNB occupation levels and building up the wall against them. This wall, built of massive stones, thus acted as a retaining wall for the growing mound of occupation debris behind it, and this may have been the reason for the wall's later collapse. It was rebuilt, and it collapsed again; and a new wall was then built 6.5 m further west to retain the spreading debris, on top of which another eight occupation levels were built. There may have been a further, similar stage of collapse and rebuilding. A clearer example of how a tell is formed could hardly be found.

For further reference

E. Anati, *Palestine before the Hebrews*, J. Cape, London, 1963.
J. Mellaart, *The Neolithic of the Near East*, Thames and Hudson, London, 1975.

S. Cole, *The Neolithic Revolution*, 5th edn., British Museum, London, 1970.

K. M. Kenyon, *Archaeology in the Holy Land*, 4th edn., Benn, London; Norton, New York, 1979.

J. Garstang and J. B. E. Garstang, *The story of Jericho*, 2nd edn., Marshall, Morgan and Scott, London, 1948.

P. Singh, *Neolithic Cultures of Western Asia*, Seminar Press, London and New York, 1974.

4

The arrival of pottery

The lengthy period of over two and a half millennia which separates PPNB Jericho from the renaissance of Jericho in the Early Bronze age is not easy to account for. Although this was an era in which first pottery and then metal objects began to be made, and though Tell es-Sultan was certainly occupied for a time, it seems that there was something of a decline in the cultural level reached, and that for a considerable period the tell was unoccupied. There is much disagreement about the interpretation of the archaeological evidence for Palestine in this period. Some scholars think of one 'Pottery Neolithic' culture existing in several regional versions, one along the Palestinian coast and Esdraelon valley, another in the north Jordan valley, and a third in Judaea and the south Jordan valley, including Jericho. Other scholars think of a 'Pottery Neolithic' or 'Late Neolithic' culture existing in three phases, the first being the 'Yarmukian' (originally recognised at Shaᶜar Ha-golan on the river Yarmuk in north Transjordan), the second and third being identical with Kenyon's Pottery Neolithic A and B (Garstang's Jericho IX and VIII) at Jericho. A further difficulty is the dating of this period and its phases. This depends largely upon the radio-carbon datings for certain sites in Syria and Lebanon (there is little such dating available for Palestinian sites) and upon the inter-relationship between the Palestinian and Syrian-Lebanese sites. Two key sites are Byblos, on the Lebanese coast, and Munhata (Horvat Minha) 9 miles south of the Sea of Galilee.

It seems clear that Jericho, with Munhata, Beidha, and other PPNB sites was abandoned at the end of PPNB, perhaps about 6000 BC. According to Kenyon, the destruction of PPNB Jericho 'is followed by a period of erosion, with the familiar wearing away of levels on the edge of the mound until the debris reached a natural angle of rest'. Many scholars think of the early sixth millennium BC as seeing the total depopulation of Palestine, and some carry this period of abandonment down to the fifth millennium BC. But most scholars are reluctant to believe that the land was empty for so long (particularly at Jericho, with its great natural advantages), and there is perhaps growing evidence for some continuity of occupation in Palestine through this period, especially in the north at Beisamun in the Huleh region and

Hagoshrim at the foot of Mount Hermon. But at Munhata and Jericho, there seems to be a clear gap between PPNB and the Pottery Neolithic period.

The earliest Pottery Neolithic level at Munhata (level 2B.2) belongs with levels excavated at Sha'ar Ha-golan and elsewhere to the 'Yarmukian' phase. It is distinguished by circular pit dwellings and silos, coarsely serrated sickle blades, axes with polished butts, incised pebble figurines, and clay female figurines with painted heads (Figure 8). The pottery was coarse, decorated with red-painted chevrons, and with a herringbone pattern incised between two lines in a zigzag form round the pot. This 'Yarmukian' culture has sometimes been seen as contemporary with Pottery Neolithic A at Jericho, but it is probably earlier. The chronological correlation between Pottery Neolithic at Jericho and at other important sites can be seen in the following simplified table.

Date	Byblos	Munhata	Jericho	Others
6000				
5500	Early Neolithic			Beisamun Hagoshrim Sha'ar Ha-golan
		2B.2		
		2B.1	IX/PNA	
5000				
	Middle Neolithic	2A	VIII/PNB	Wadi Rabah
4500				
	Late Neolithic			
4000				

When Garstang excavated Jericho in 1931–5 he dug into the Pottery Neolithic levels, and on the evidence of the two main types of pottery found he distinguished between the earlier stratum IX and the later stratum VIII. From Garstang's Jericho IX came two sorts of pottery. The first was a coarse ware – flat-based bowls with straight sides and jars with curved walls – in which the clay was bound with chopped straw, and the surface finished by being smoothed with grass, which left clear traces of its use. The second type was finer, the surface covered with a cream coloured slip on which triangular and diamond designs were painted in red slip, which was burnished, leaving a pattern of cream coloured chevrons and zigzags. In Garstang's stratum VIII, this painted pottery yielded to better fired pottery, which used no straw, and was finished by being turned on a mat. It was incised with herringbone patterns, and was distinguished by a rim which is

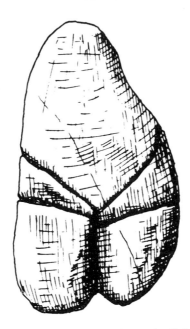

Figure 8   A Neolithic pebble figurine from Shaᶜar ha-Golan (after Stekelis).

concave internally and convex externally and so called 'bow rim' pottery. Its handles are loops, whose ends widen where they join the body of the pot. This pottery is also represented at Munhata 2A and Wadi Rabah (Figure 9).

Kenyon assigned these two main types of pottery, from Jericho IX and VIII, to two groups of people, Pottery Neolithic A and Pottery Neolithic B, and she further connected them with different architectural stages at Jericho. But she noted that the second type of pottery (Jericho VIII/PNB) could be linked with the pottery from Shaᶜar Ha-golan and with similar material from the Early and Middle Neolithic stages at Byblos. Probably this fashion, with its herringbone pattern, reached Jericho from the north via Shaᶜar Ha-golan, after it had become standard there. This PNB style, according to R. de Vaux, is found associated with Yarmukian influence in the lower levels of several tells of northern Palestine, and in particular it is associated with pit-dwellings (e.g., Bethshan, Balata, Tell el-Farᶜah). The Jericho IX/PNA style, however, tends to be found mostly at sites on the coastal plains of Palestine (e.g., Tell Batashi, Wadi Rabah, Lydda). This has suggested that this PNA pottery represents a regional culture contemporary with PNB. However, the geographical distinction is not complete, for both PNA and PNB appear together at Megiddo and at Jericho, and at Jericho, as Kenyon has noted, there is some stratigraphic overlap between the two. The geographical and chronological relationships of PNA and PNB, therefore, remain far from clear. The Jericho evidence is ambiguous because, though

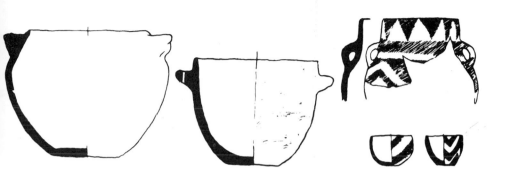

Figure 9   Neolithic pottery from Jericho (after Ben Dor and Kenyon).

there are clear indications of more than one occupation period in Pottery Neolithic, it is not easy to assign the finds (including the different types of pottery) to particular periods. This is because much of the material comes from the pit-dwellings which contain material from the Pre-pottery Neolithic levels into which the pits were originally dug, material from the levels destroyed when the pits were dug, and material from the people who actually dug the pits.

In addition to pottery, these Pottery Neolithic levels at Jericho contained also stone tools and weapons. Distinctive were the sickle blades, 3–4 cms long, retouched at both ends, with a coarse denticulation; they were possibly used for cutting reeds rather than gathering ears of corn. Arrow heads were small – perhaps for smaller game and birds rather than for the larger game – 3–4 cms long, with pointed tangs and tips. Scrapers were wide knives of tabular flint, retouched along the cutting edge. Polished axes became common. The fine querns, pestles and stone bowls of PPNB, however, are no longer used. There seems to be little evidence, in fact, for either plants or animals in this period, though emmer, barley and einkhorn were still gathered. The few animal bones found were mainly sheep and goat, which presumably provided the main meat supply (as at Munhata, where these animals seem to have been ousting the gazelle).

The history of occupation at Jericho in the Pottery Neolithic period is shown best by the sequence of attempts at housing. We have already mentioned the evidence for the decay and erosion of the PPNB strata of the tell. Towards the summit of the tell, however, among the ruins of the PPNB occupation, there were remains of earthen floors and hearths, which seem to have belonged to the immediate successors of the PPNB people on the site. There are no walls visible that can be related to those floors, and perhaps their makers camped on them without benefit of solid roofing over their heads. In places, several successive floor levels survive. Possibly these floors were the work of the earlier generations of Pottery Neolithic A people. Whoever made the floors, they were succeeded by people who cut pits through the floors into the PPNB levels below. (Elsewhere, on the steeper slopes of the tell, where the floors do not appear, the pits were cut directly into the PPNB levels.) The pits were at first interpreted as quarries for mud-brick, but comparison with other sites of the period has shown that these were semi-subterranean dwellings. The edges of these pits were strengthened by walling of mud and stone, and the roofs were probably made of mud and branches. The pits were up to 2 metres deep and 3 metres in diameter. Their floors show a succession of occupation levels and hearths, but how long these pit-dwellings were the standard housing on this site we do not know. Kenyon ascribes these pits to the PNA people. At Munhata 2B.1 similar dwellings are found, built of bun-shaped bricks set on stone foundations. These were followed in the next phase at Munhata (2A) by rectangular houses. At Jericho, the PNB people built similar houses, probably rectangular (though some of the walls seem to have been curved), with stone foundations and upper layers made of 'bun-shaped' (plano-convex) round bricks. Associated with a second phase of such buildings was a large wall, 2.25 metres broad, of which a length of 19 metres was found; this may have been part of the city wall of the period. There were also stone-walled buildings from a slightly later period.

Chronologically, all this is not very satisfactory. There seem to have been perhaps two phases of PNA people and three (?) of PNB people, possibly with some overlapping between PNA and PNB. The latter have a new pottery tradition, but appear to build on the former's dwellings. The PNB people therefore do not differ from the PNA people in their architectural tradition, though their architecture changes and develops with time. The use of circular pit-dwellings is reminiscent of the earlier Neolithic period, and their semi-subterranean nature perhaps points forward to the subterranean dwellings of the following Chalcolithic period in the Negev. Possibly we are dealing once again with a people who are in process of changing their way of life from semi-nomadic to a more settled way of life. How long all this took is not clear, but the PNA and PNB periods at Jericho probably belong somewhere between 5500 and 4000 BC. The archaeological evidence suggests that the site was abandoned or partly abandoned for a period both before and after its occupation by the Pottery Neolithic peoples, though this does not necessarily mean that the Jericho region was totally lacking in population. But this Pottery Neolithic period, though it knew the art of making useful and durable vessels of clay instead of shaping them laboriously from stone, seems to have been in some ways a less advanced community than its Pre-pottery Neolithic predecessors. Perhaps the picture will change if ever burials from this period are discovered. We have the under-floor burials and plastered skulls from the Pre-pottery Neolithic B period, and the rock-cut tombs from the following Bronze ages, but, strangely, nothing at all from the Pottery Neolithic period. The dead may have been buried in some cemetery yet to be found, or perhaps cremated, or perhaps simply exposed in the wilderness outside the community. Evidence of how these people disposed of their dead might extend our knowledge of the period considerably.

The historical connection between Pottery Neolithic Jericho and subsequent occupation of the site needs much more research and probably much more evidence than is at present available. Kenyon states that Pottery Neolithic Jericho was followed by a period of abandonment, demonstrated in Trench I by a level of humus formed by natural deposit. In this case it seems that the tell was, in this section at least, not eroded but built up. According to F. E. Zeuner (*Palestine Exploration Quarterly* (1954), pp. 64–68), the amount of time needed for such a deposit to develop was (to judge from more modern examples) not less than 300 years. What happened on one part of the tell, however, may not have happened on another, and in the period after Pottery Neolithic and before the next occupation, perhaps c. 3300 BC, the tell may have been occupied only in part. This period, covering most of the fourth millennium BC, is usually described as the Chalcolithic period, for it is an age which saw the introduction of the use of copper, while continuing to use tools and implements of flint and other stone. More specifically, this period in Palestine is often called 'Ghassulian', taking its name from a site called Teleilat Ghassul, which lies at the south end of the Jordan valley, a few miles east of Jericho across the river Jordan. Related sites have been found in the Negev. Near Beersheba, for example, people lived in subterranean chambers, and worked copper mined at Feinan sixty miles away. A magnificent hoard of over 400 copper objects of great splendour was found in a cave in Nahal Mishmar. This culture is certainly one of the most fascinating to have arisen in pre-Israelite Palestine.

Little trace of Ghassulian artefacts has been found at Tell es-Sultan (though some traces have been found at Tulul abu el-ᶜalaiq nearby), and this negative evidence has supported the belief that Tell es-Sultan was unoccupied for most of the fourth millennium BC. There are, however, signs at Jericho in the later Pottery Neolithic material of some links with the Ghassulian culture and so perhaps of transition to the Chalcolithic period. Garstang found jars with rims bearing finger impressions and with additionally applied strips of clay round the body. There was also part of a 'cornet' cup and a fragment of a basalt bowl with a hatched triangle incised below the rim. These are Ghassulian features. There were also flints typical of the Ghassulian period – in particular, steeply backed sickle blades and tabular flint fan scrapers. Some of the technical features of Jericho's Pottery Neolithic pottery are perhaps the forerunners of common features of Chalcolithic pottery; for example, some Pottery Neolithic B pots had on their base the mark of the spiral design of the mat on which they were made, and the same thing appears on the base of Chalcolithic pottery, though in this case the pattern is criss-cross. The 'hole-mouth jar', whose mouth is a wide hole in the flattened top of a roughly globular jar, appears first in Pottery Neolithic and later in Chalcolithic. A band of red paint is used on the rims of Pottery Neolithic bowls and is still used in the Chalcolithic period.

What this means for the history of Jericho in the fourth millennium BC needs some consideration. The end of the Pottery Neolithic period may perhaps be dated to the second half of the fifth millennium BC. Sometime in this period there was a transition to the Ghassulian period; Teleilat Ghassul itself apparently developed from Late Neolithic beginnings in the mid-fifth millennium BC and came to an end towards the mid-fourth millennium BC. There is pottery evidence of Ghassulian occupation at Tell es-Sultan, and also at nearby Tulul abu el-ᶜalaiq, and at Tell Ghanam and El-adeimeh a few miles east across the Jordan. But there are no known Ghassulian building levels or structure at Tell es-Sultan, and the humus deposit in Trench I suggests a gap in occupation, at least in that part of the tell, for about 300 years or more. We may probably conclude that in a time of changing economic and social conditions, Jericho may simply have become a less popular place in which to live, and people moved to other places. The Chalcolithic period in southern Palestine was not a period of towns and cities so much as of small villages and communities, living without benefit of walls and defences. Jericho came into her own again in the following urban period of the Early Bronze age, heralded by what Kenyon has called the 'Proto-Urban' age.

For further reference

Ruth Amiran, *Ancient Pottery of the Holy Land*, Rutgers University Press, 1970.

E. Anati, *Palestine before the Hebrews*, Jonathan Cape, London, 1963.

J. Mellaart, *The Neolithic of the Near East*, Thames and Hudson, London, 1975.

K. M. Kenyon, *Archaeology in the Holy Land*, 4th ed., Benn, London; Norton, New York, 1979.

J. Garstang and J. B. E. Garstang, *The story of Jericho*, 2nd edn., Marshall, Morgan and Scott, London, 1948.

K. M. Kenyon, *Digging up Jericho*, Benn, London, 1957.

R. de Vaux, 'Palestine during the Neolithic and Chalcolithic Periods', in *Cambridge Ancient History*, 3rd edn., vol. I, ch. IX(b), § v-viii, Cambridge, 1970, pp. 499–538.

5

Jericho in the Bronze Age

Proto-Urban Jericho

The next stage of Jericho's history is known primarily from a small number of tombs cut from the rock in the sides of minor wadis to the northwest of the tell, and from a limited number of building remains on the north end of the tell itself. On the tell there are four, or perhaps five, structural phases belonging to this period, in the following sequence,

Q   huge buildings (one with an apse at the end) of mudbrick on heavy stone foundations, with a terrace wall and courtyard

P,O rebuilding activities

N   a new building, followed by earthquake (?) destruction

M   complete rebuilding; the phase ends with the collapse of the terrace wall and subsequent temporary abandonment of the site.

From the pottery and other finds, these phases have been associated with tombs A13, A61, A94, A114, A124, A130 and K1, K2 ('A' referring to areas about 700 m north of the tell, and 'K' to an area about 300 m northwest of the tell). These tombs had been excavated to provide space for multiple burials. On the present evidence, almost 800 people were buried in these few tombs, together with various grave goods. In all cases the original roof has disappeared, probably as the result of erosion in the third millennium BC. But most of the tombs' original contents were preserved under the debris of the collapse and subsequent infill.

The oldest tomb is probably A94, radio-carbon dated to 3260 ± 110 BC. It contained a large number of wide, shallow, hand-made bowls and bulbous juglets whose handles were looped up a little above the level of the rim of the pot (Plate 10). There were larger jars with ledge handles, some with spouts, including one distinctive jar with a spout and a pair of loop handles on the sides. The ware is generally reddish in colour, and burnished. Various beads (originally decorating the corpses), a copper or bronze ring, a few flint

Plate 10   Proto-Urban A pottery from Jericho, Tomb A94.

blades, and a burnt piece of what was probably textile, complete the inventory. The centre of the tomb revealed a lower fill of red earth levelling the floor, above which were alternate layers of burnt material and rock chips. It seems that there was a sequence of fires cremating human long bones. The skulls (113 of them) were placed round the fire in a circle facing inwards, and they show signs of scorching. After the cremation was over, the bulk of the pottery was put in round the edge and the tomb was deliberately filled in. The bodies had apparently been allowed to decay until the heads could be removed. This is reminiscent of earlier practice at Jericho, and one must perhaps suppose that the tradition of preserving the skull separately from the body died hard at Jericho. The excavation of similar tombs, however, showed that only in A94 was cremation used to dispose of the bones; elsewhere, most of the bones and pottery goods were probably thrown out (and burnt elsewhere?) as the bodies decayed, to leave room for others, the skulls alone being preserved in the tomb. The pottery in A94, and other similar tombs, commonly described as red-burnished ware, finds parallels in the earliest tombs of Tell el-Farʿah near Nablus, at Tell en-Nasbeh, at Ai, and also at sites in Galilee and Transjordan and in the Beersheba region. Further connections have been demonstrated with north Syria, Cilicia and Anatolia. From Palestine, the influence of this material reached into Egypt. Kenyon named this culture 'Proto-Urban A'.

Another Jericho tomb in which this Proto-Urban A culture appeared was A13. But above the Proto-Urban A remains of levels IV–III were levels II–I which each contained stone pavements with associated bones and (in level II) one skull. The pottery here, however, was quite different, including bowls and jars with a highly distinctive geometric decoration of red painted lines. In tomb K2 there were two similar phases, the first clearly Proto-Urban A (though later than that of tomb A94) and the second containing the beautifully decorated pottery of A13's upper levels (Figure 10). This second phase was designated Proto-Urban B by Kenyon, and similar material was found at Tell en-Nasbeh, Ai, Ophel (Jerusalem), and in smaller quantities at Tell el-Farʿah. In the central highland region north of Jerusalem, Proto-Urban A and B appear to be contemporary. However, the Jericho evidence of the tombs and of the tell (where Proto-Urban B appears only in the later phases O, N, M described above and not in the earlier Q,P) suggests that at Jericho at least Proto-Urban B arrived later than Proto-Urban A. But the Proto-Urban B material does not seem to occur apart from Proto-Urban A, and the groups of people who produced these different groups of pottery must be fairly closely related.

The picture is complicated, however, by the presence of a third group of pottery often known as 'Esdraelon ware' and identified by Kenyon as 'Proto-Urban C'. This pottery appears with Proto-Urban A pottery at Tell

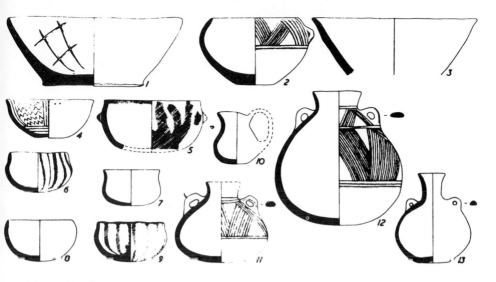

Figure 10   Proto-Urban B pottery from Jericho, Tomb A13.

el-Farᶜah, Megiddo and other places, and perhaps belongs to a group pene-
trating Palestine from the north via the Esdraelon plain, its ultimate origin
being perhaps Anatolia. Both the clay and the highly burnished slip of this
pottery are grey. This pottery does not appear in the Jericho tombs or on
the tell, apart from one imitation in phase II of tomb K2, but it does appear
nearby at Tulul abu el-ᶜalaiq.

It is clear that these three groups of pottery are roughly contemporary,
and also that they overlap to some extent with the Chalcolithic material
found in the Beersheba region, Megiddo, Bethshan and elsewhere. De Vaux
stresses the contemporaneity of the Proto-Urban C culture with the
Ghassulian-Beersheba culture, and sees this pottery as representing the villages of the farmers, potters and metal-workers of the Chalcolithic era. Only
the Proto-Urban B painted ware, the last of this group to appear, might
herald the coming Early Bronze age. G. E. Wright and Ruth Amiran,
however, see these red- and grey-burnished wares as belonging basically to
the new Early Bronze age, while Kathleen Kenyon takes a middle view.
These different pottery groups represent groups of people invading Palestine
via the Esdraelon plain and Jericho, meeting in the central Tell el-Farᶜah
region. They established regional cultures. At Jericho they lived side by side
on two separate sites, perhaps hostile towards one another (for there is little
sign of mutual influence). They lived as villagers rather than as town-dwell-
ers; at Jericho they occupied only a small, undefended part of the tell. There

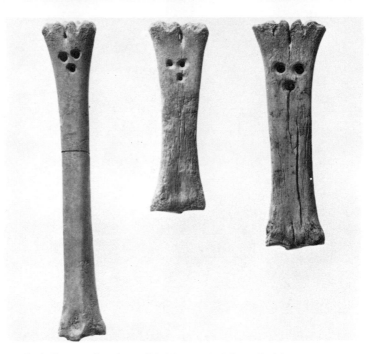

Plate 11   Early Bronze Age bone 'idols' or 'dolls' from Jericho.

is little about these people which might make us think of them as 'urban' in
their habits, but on the ground that it was from the sites they occupied that
the walled towns of the Early Bronze age developed, Kenyon argues that
the peoples represented by this pottery should be called 'Proto-Urban'. On
the evidence of tomb A94 they were settled round Jericho c. 3300 BC. The
transition to the Early Bronze age took place over the following centuries.

Early Bronze Age Jericho

It is surprising how little we know of the Early Bronze age (c. 3100–2300
BC) at Jericho. This was a period when writing was known and practised in
Mesopotamia and Egypt, and historical records of a sort begin to appear.
Writing, however, had not yet appeared in Palestine; the nearest we get to
it at Jericho is perhaps a bone cylinder from an Early Bronze tomb, incised
with a design and reminiscent of a Mesopotamian cylinder seal. In Palestine,
this was a period when the walled city became common, particularly in the
northern part of the country and on sites occupied by Kenyon's Proto-Urban
peoples (e.g., Tell el-Farᶜah, Megiddo, Bethshan, Ai, Jerusalem, Gezer).
The Early Bronze life-style evolved out of the Proto-Urban, perhaps with

68

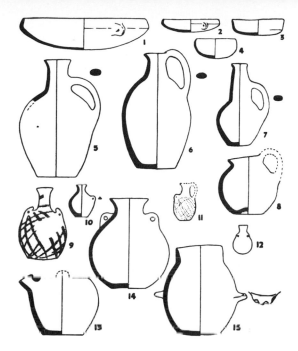

Figure 11   Pottery from early in the Early Bronze Age, Jericho, Tomb A108.

the help of further immigrants from the north, behind whom lay the stimulus of the coastal towns of Syria. Further south, the region of the Ghassulian-Beersheba cultures, the rise of cities on the whole does not happen until later (Early Bronze III), and further south still signs of city life are absent. There is no sign of Early Bronze settlement in the Negev, apart from Arad, which has EB I and II levels.

What distinguishes cities of the Early Bronze period from the settlements of the later Neolithic and Chalcolithic periods is the existence of solid defence ramparts and walls, which seem to become more solid as the period advances. Towers were known and used, as at Arad and Jerusalem, Ai and Jericho, and these early towers are perhaps pictured on the Egyptian 'Narmer Palette' (though as Narmer was contemporary with the Proto-Urban period, the palette may picture fortified towns of the Egyptian delta rather than of southern Palestine). There was a fair amount of contact between Palestine and Egypt in the Early Bronze period, evidenced at EB I Jericho by a black stone palette with lines incised round the edge, of a style current in late pre-Dynastic or Dynasty I Egypt. In Egypt under Dynasty I, 'Abydos' ware seems first to have been imported from Palestine before the local potters began to make it for themselves; some of this ware was found at Jericho.

The real contacts of the Early Bronze age, however, as is shown by the

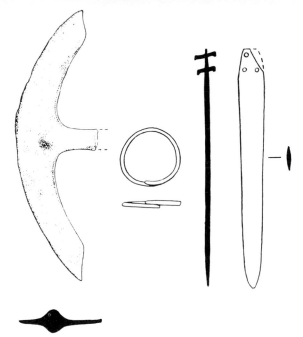

Figure 12   Crescentic axehead from Jericho, Tomb A114(B) and dagger from tomb F5. The axehead may be dated *c.* 2400 – 2200 BC.

pottery, were with Syria, and, beyond that, with Anatolia. The potter's art advanced greatly in the Early Bronze age, as he learned to use the wheel to shape the rim of the vessel more accurately (he did not yet use a fast wheel to shape the whole pot), and a new form of kiln with two chambers, one above the other. The fire was laid in the lower chamber, and the sun-dried pots put in the upper, producing better-shaped and better-fired pots, some gaining a hard 'metallic' quality. The pottery has a distinctive red burnish, often vertically down the sides of the pot rather than horizontally across it. Bands of red or brown colour are used as decoration. In the early period, typical were hole-mouth jars (sometimes up to 3ft high), and dishes or bowls with carination and an in-curving rim (Figure 11). Profiles changed as the millennium proceeded; rounder-bottomed bowls became flat-bottomed, bag-shaped juglets disappeared and piriform juglets became common; new types of jug arrived with stump-bases (like a Staffordshire pottery kiln upside down).

Although the period is called 'Early Bronze', bronze in fact hardly appears, and was not common. The nine Early Bronze tombs at Jericho reveal only some copper wire, a ring, some beads, two bracelet fragments, a dagger, and a crescentic axehead (Figure 12) paralleled by one from Tell el-Hesi, where the collection included six flat axes and two spearheads. A much

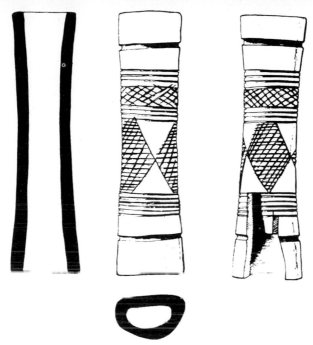

Figure 13   Bone object from Early Bronze III, Jericho, Tomb F4.

better idea of the copper industry is given by the hoard from Kfar Monash (between Tel Aviv and Haifa), which contained daggers, spearheads, a mace, what are probably scales of breastplate armour, and tools such as axes, adzes, chisels, and knives. This belonged to EB I–II; the workmanship was local, the metal at least in part imported from Anatolia. At Megiddo were found moulds for casting axes. But the use of flint and bone tools continued (particularly common were trapezoidal flint blades which, with their edges serrated, were used for sickles), and copper was probably beyond the means of most ordinary people, who were perhaps prosperous enough but not wealthy. There is not much evidence of imported goods. It is not clear what Palestine could have exported in return, except perhaps pottery and olive oil.

Early Bronze Jericho as revealed by excavation fits well into this general picture of third millennium BC Palestine. In the north central area of the tell (sites E III and IV) a series of building phases was excavated. Phases Q–M, as we have seen, belonged to the 'Proto-Urban' period; phases L–K, containing very little by way of architectural remains but perhaps providing the first examples of walled, sunken storage silos, belonged to EB I. Phase J introduced a new architectural tradition and a new period in the site's history which was continued in phases H and G; this belonged to EB II. To this period belong the broad platters and the stump-base jugs and juglets, and jars with tall, cylindrical necks and column handles. Phases F and E saw the levelling of the area, and the introduction of a brick pavement, brick silos, and the setting of cylindrical storage jars in the floor with their mouths at ground level. Phase D saw a major reconstruction and phase C a major break in the city's history. In phase C there were no buildings over most of the area excavated, though continuity with the previous phases E and D was still evident in the sunken jars (which now had brick collars built round their necks) and the brick silos. Phases B and A had a completely new lay-out. Phases F–D mark the first half of EB III, and phases C–A the second. Further north, this EB III period was marked by 'Khirbet Kerak' ware – handsome red and black pottery, burnished, with incised decoration, named after the site south of the Sea of Galilee where it was first found. This ware is found chiefly in the region of Bethshan and the Esdraelon valley, and is absent from sites E III and IV at Jericho, though it is found in some later EB tombs (e.g. F4, F2). The pottery of phases F–D on the tell shows the stump-bases becoming taller and narrower, and in phases C–A we find broad platters and bowls with sharply inturned rims.

It is not clear just how this sequence of building phases relates to the seventeen phases of building and rebuilding which affected the town wall of the period. This building activity does not mean that EB Jericho was de-stroyed and rebuilt seventeen times, for many of these rebuildings may have been the repair of natural decay or of earthquake damage. At one point the wall was built with vertical section gaps, perhaps to limit the damage done by earthquakes or tremors.

The line of the EB walls on the north and west sides of the tell is known, but on the east side it is not. The eastern walls were lower, coming down close to the spring and perhaps enclosing it, and they have been eroded away and finally destroyed by the development of the road which passes along the eastern foot of the tell. Garstang found what might have been a tower or gateway of the EB wall, at the foot of the mounds towards the southeast corner. On the north end of the tell, the EB wall ran along what had become the crest of the mound (Plate 12), 100ft or so south of the line of the Pre-pottery Neolithic walls, and similarly at the south end, the wall ran 84ft inside the earlier walls. The walled area of the EB town was therefore probably rather smaller than that of the Pre-pottery Neolithic town, covering about 8 acres compared with the previous 10. The best evidence, however, for the sequence of the EB walls was found in Kenyon's Trench I on the west side of the tell (Figure 14). It was this trench which showed clearly that the walls which Garstang thought made a double Late Bronze wall really represented two different stages of the EB defences. In fact there were

Plate 12　The Early Bronze Age wall at its highest point in the north-west corner of Tell es-Sultan.

JERICHO *TRENCH 1*

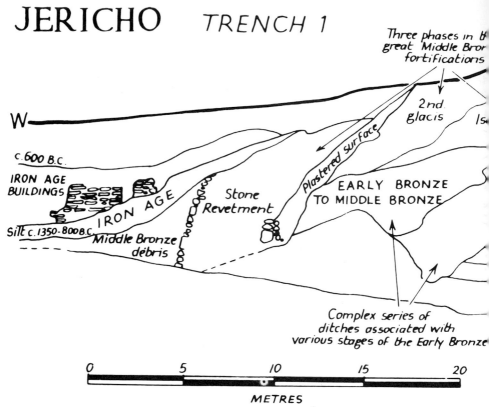

Figure 14   A simplified drawing of the north section of Kenyon's Trench I at Tell
es-Sultan, showing the relationship of the Early Bronze and Middle
Bronze town walls.

several stages, not all visible in the section drawn of the sides of Trench I.
The history of the EB walls on the west side of the tell may be summarised
as follows,

1. The earliest EB wall (A), 1.20 m thick, was built with its foundations cutting
   directly into the Pottery Neolithic strata. This wall appears to have had a
   circular tower associated with it. This wall was rebuilt several times.
2. The wall was doubled by the addition of a new wall (B) behind it.
3. The outer wall (A) collapsed and was rebuilt.
4. A new wall (C) was added on the outside to support (A). The resultant triple
   wall was now 3.4 metres wide.
5. After a history of collapses and repairs, the triple wall was finally abandoned.
6. A massive new wall (D) was built inside the line of walls A, B, and C. It was
   made of larger bricks (12 × 75 × 45 cms) and was associated with a ditch 12.5
   metres in front of it down the slope. At some stage it was destroyed, then
   rebuilt, and later destroyed or abandoned.

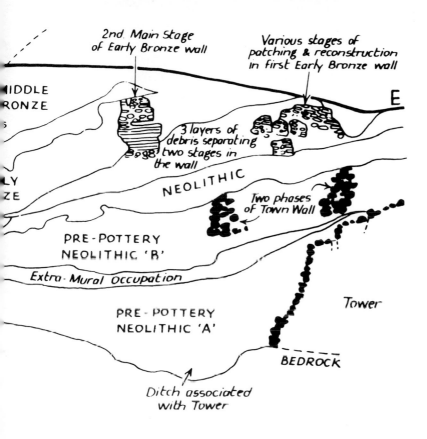

2nd Main Stage of Early Bronze wall

Various stages of patching & reconstruction in first Early Bronze wall

E

MIDDLE BRONZE

3 layers of debris separating two stages in the wall

NEOLITHIC

Two phases of Town Wall

LY ZE

PRE-POTTERY NEOLITHIC 'B'

Extra-Mural Occupation

PRE-POTTERY NEOLITHIC 'A'

Tower

BEDROCK

Ditch associated with Tower

7. Yet another wall (E) was now built, though after a gap long enough to leave three layers of debris on top of the old wall D. The new wall E was placed 8 metres down the slope, and its foundations cut into the three layers of debris just mentioned. This was thus clearly not contemporary with wall D – a discovery which disproved Garstang's identification of these two walls as a double wall of the Late Bronze period. Wall E was thus not sited at the top of the slope; it was cut into the surface of the slope. The town at this period was terraced up behind the wall, which probably acted in part as a retaining wall. It collapsed at least once and was repaired.

8. A new wall (F) was built on top of E, apparently in great haste, with lower courses of rough stones and rubble, and upper works of loosely-laid mud-brick. This was perhaps thrown up as a protection against the sudden appearance of the people responsible for the end of EB Jericho. The wall was destroyed by fire, the brick being burnt to a red colour from one side of the wall to the other. Outside the wall there were layers of ash from the wood that had been piled up against the wall, and inside the layers of burning show that the attack succeeded in setting fire to the town inside.

Of the political events which resulted in the destruction of EB Jericho in the EB III period we know nothing. As one of the cities of EB Palestine, Jericho was probably independent and self-governing. She might have provoked the enmity of another city, though this seems unlikely, as Jericho had no obvious rivals. It is more likely that Jericho was attacked by semi-settled inhabitants of surrounding areas, who resented Jericho's control of the fertile land of the valley. Kenyon suggested that Jericho was significantly weakened economically by the erosion caused in the third millennium BC by extensive deforestation of the area. Evidence of this is seen both in the large quantity of wood used in EB Jericho (seen in tomb finds), and in the erosion visible in the roofless EB tombs along the wadis. This erosion took place before the tombs of the subsequent Intermediate Early Bronze – Middle Bronze period were dug, and can therefore be dated to the second half of the third millennium BC. But how much of the topsoil of the Jericho region disappeared in erosion in these centuries is hard to say. Deforestation, however, would certainly lead to the diminution of game that could be caught locally. Economic circumstances surely played their part in the decline and fall of EB Jericho, but the details remain a matter for speculation.

Intermediate Early Bronze – Middle Bronze Age Jericho

It is not possible to give a precise date for the end of the Early Bronze age. Archaeologists are not agreed on the length of the period that can properly be described as 'Early Bronze', some dividing it into four main periods (EB I, II, III, IV), others into three only, reckoning EB IV as part of an intermediate period between EB and MB. There is similar disagreement about the beginning of the Middle Bronze age, resulting in some confusion of nomenclature. Thus what American archaeologists (following W. F. Albright) usually call MB I is ascribed by British archaeologists to what Kenyon (following J. H. Iliffe) called 'Intermediate EB–MB', and the American MB IIA has become the British MB I. The position may be stated in a small table,

	Albright and others	*Kenyon and others*
2400 BC	EB IV (or IIIB)	
2300		Intermediate EB-MB
2200		
2100	MB I	
2000		
1900	MB IIA	MB I
1800		MB II

76

Plate 13 Intermediate Early Bronze-Middle Bronze lamp, jars and 'tea-pot' from Jericho.

The major point at issue is not so much the naming and dating of the different periods, though there is some variation between scholars, but the nature of the different periods. Kenyon's terminology underlines that this period belongs neither to the EB nor to the succeeding MB civilisation. It was rather the result of the invasion of a new group of people, with new ways of life, whom Kenyon calls 'Amorites' and relates to the Sumerian Martu and Akkadian Amurru, known from Mesopotamian texts to be making their presence felt throughout the Fertile Crescent at this time. Other scholars have argued that though newcomers (perhaps 'Amorites') entered Palestine at the end of EB, the culture they brought had its links with the

Syrian EB culture, the pottery forms brought by these newcomers in particular being 'survivals from an adaptation of the EB forms' (G. E. Wright). More recently, it has become clear that the Intermediate EB–MB culture derives from the combination of the indigenous EB traditions and innovating traditions brought by people coming from the Euphrates region of north Syria. In the pottery of this period, the use of flat bases, ledge handles, comb decoration, hole-mouth cooking pots and deep bowls continues the EB tradition, while the disappearance of the typical EB red slip and burnishing, and the appearance of such new forms as lamps, cups, bowls with grooves at the rim, globular jugs with pinched mouths, and of a finer, thinner pottery, suggests the presence of people from places like Mari, Harran, Til Barsip and Hammam in northern Syria (Plate 13). At Jericho, Kenyon notes that the flat bases are now very thin and roughly finished underneath, and that the ledge handles have their edges folded right over. The pottery has a harsh, gritty texture, and is decorated with incised straight and wavy lines. A similar combination of indigenous and imported tradition is seen in the metal objects – daggers, javelins, axes, pins – of this period. The metal used is mainly copper, though bronze is beginning to appear.

It has usually been said that the people of this period were nomadic or at least semi-nomadic, and Kenyon argued that for at least two centuries (c. 2200–2000 BC) Tell es-Sultan was a campsite rather than a town. Yet these people were not entirely without buildings. There is evidence for rectangular buildings with stone foundations and mud-brick walls at a number of sites either side of the Jordan, and at Jericho, after an interval of time indicated by a 2.75 m layer of silt above the w-shaped ditch fronting the EB town wall, houses were built on terraces on the slopes of the tell. (On the top, however, the MB levels follow directly on the EB levels.) In Trench I, on the west side of the tell, a two-roomed building was cut back into the slope. Inside were two structures which may have been altars (built into one was an intact cup). Below the wall of one room, in which there was a clay bin perhaps designed for offerings, was the remains of an infant in a bag, possibly a foundation sacrifice. The building perhaps had religious significance.

From the remaining evidence, however, the skill and industry of the Intermediate EB–MB people was employed not on building houses (which seem to have been of poor quality) but on excavating tombs. 346 are known, yielding a total of 356 individuals buried. Unlike the EB tombs, these were cut for individual, not group burial (Figure 15). As this might involve the excavation and removal of up to fifty or more tons of rock for each tomb, clearly these people thought such burial an important matter.

There are five major different types of these tombs at Jericho, some of

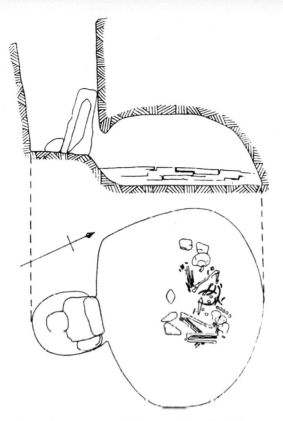

Figure 15   Plan of Jericho Tomb A111 (Intermediate Early Bronze – Middle
Bronze period).

which, with variations, are paralleled at other Intermediate EB–MB sites.
The 'dagger tombs' (105 in all) consist of a 1.5 m diameter chamber, entered
by a vertical circular shaft 1–2 m deep. The body, on its side in a contracted
position, was accompanied by a copper dagger with central rib and rivetted
handle (women were accompanied by a copper pin and some beads). Quite
distinct were the 158 'pottery tombs', whose shafts were 2 m in diameter
and 3–4 m deep, and whose chambers were up to 3 m long. The skeletons
were incomplete, the bones having probably been collected and deposited in
the tomb only after the flesh had decayed. With them were 5–20 pottery
jars, possibly deliberately made for funerary purposes, for the type, with
round body and straight neck, does not appear in contemporary levels on
the tell. The 4 'square-shaft' tombs contained intact skeletons, with offerings
similar to those in the 'pottery tombs'. The 15 or 16 'bead tombs' contained
disarticulated skeletons with beads 'as the most generally found deposit',
though in fact beads (of carnelian) are listed among the finds of only three

of these tombs. More striking were the 'outsize tombs', with rectangular shafts 3 m wide and 5 m deep, and chambers 6.3 × 3.3 m in area and 2.6 m high. The pottery is similar to that of the 'pottery tombs', though new types (ledge-handled jars, and 'tea-pots', i.e., ledge-handled jars with spouts) appear in some tombs. Lamps were placed on the floor, though niches had been cut for them in the walls. This practice with the lamp may be all that remained of an original custom of providing light for the dead. Similarly, the presence of animal bones strewn across the tomb (only the poorer joints of sheep or goat were found) may represent the original practice of leaving food for the dead.

These different tomb-types may derive from different groups of people. The 'dagger tombs' may represent the earliest of these groups, but the 'pottery tombs' suggest the continuance of the semi-nomadic custom of secondary burial and might represent a group contemporary with the 'dagger tomb' group. If the 'bead tombs' contained the poorer relatives, as has been suggested, of the 'pottery tomb' people, the 'outsize tombs' might have contained the richer relatives. But it seems unlikely that every Jerichoan was given an expensively cut rock tomb. 346 individuals (it being granted that not all burials have been discovered) are surely a small proportion of the population of Jericho in these three or four centuries. The poorer people were probably buried with less expense. In the twentieth century BC Pharaoh Sesostris I wrote to the self-exiled courtier Sinuhe urging him to return to Egypt, and he ends by saying,

> You shall not die in a foreign land, and Asiatics will not escort you. You shall not be placed in a ram's skin as they make your grave.

Pharaoh is presumably contrasting Egyptian burial customs with the lowlier customs of Asiatics in Palestine.

The evidence from the Intermediate EB–MB Jericho tombs and tell can be compared with similar evidence from other contemporary sites such as Tell el-Ajjul, Tell ed-Duweir, Tell Beit Mirsim in the southwest, el-Jib and the Mount of Olives in the central hills, and Megiddo and Bethshan in the north. The evidence is complicated, and its interpretation uncertain. According to Ruth Amiran, the pottery evidence suggests three main groups in Palestine – a southern group, a northern group, and a third 'Megiddo' group. The Jericho tombs suggest that several different but related tribal traditions were maintained side by side, and similar, but not quite identical traditions appear further west at Tell el-Ajjul and other contemporary sites in the south. Kenyon earlier argued that related groups of people entered Palestine via Jericho and that with the passing of time and the westward movement of settlement, the different traditions overlapped and intermingled. But Jericho, rather than being the centre from which Intermediate EB–MB civilisation spread into Palestine, was more likely influenced by both northern and southern traditions, Megiddo in particular being the link with the north. There is little evidence to suggest that Palestine was invaded across the Jordan via Jericho at the beginning of this period. The association of the pottery and metal artefacts with Syria, and the distribution of Intermediate EB–MB sites, suggest rather that the population infiltrated from Syria, not necessarily via Transjordan.

Palestine at the end of the second millennium BC should not be thought of as a deserted, barren land barely populated by destitute nomads. The Intermediate EB–MB people may have used the land less intensively than the Early Bronze city-dwellers, but they acquired their food in much the same way. They hunted the gazelle, and reared sheep, goat, ox and cattle. They grew and ate barley and wheat, with peas, lentils and chickpeas, though Jericho produced no evidence from this period of the vine and fig, which require careful attention over a number of years, or of a number of other plants (e.g., flax, dates, onions) found in EB and MB Jericho. But things improved as Palestine entered the MB age, as can be seen from the description of life in Syria and Palestine left us by the Egyptian courtier Sinuhe,

There were cultivated figs in it, and grapes, and more wine than water. Its honey was abundant, and its olive trees numerous. On its trees were all varieties of fruit. There were emmer corn and barley, and there was no end to all the varieties of cattle . . . I obtained rations as daily disbursements and wine as a daily requirement, cooked meat and roasted birds, beside the desert game. They hunted for me and they set (food) down before me, in addition to the catch of my hunting dogs. They made for me many sweet things and milk boiled in every fashion ('The Story of Sinuhe,' in W. K. Simpson (ed.) *The Literature of Ancient Egypt*, New York, 1973, p. 63).

Even if this refers to Syria rather than Palestine, much of what is said could apply to Palestine. One is reminded of the biblical description of the land in Deuteronomy 8:7–9.

As we have seen, in the Early Bronze age there was a certain amount of contact between Egypt and Palestine. The last two centuries of the third millennium saw a decline in Egypt's presence in Palestine and Syria, which the Egyptians attributed to the invasion of the 'Asiatics'. The incoming aliens are described by a Pharaoh of Dynasty X (*c.* 2130–2040 BC) in his instructions to his son Merikare,

The wretched Asiatic, unpleasant is the place where he is, (with) trouble from water, difficulty from many trees, and the roads thereof awkward by reason of mountains. He does not dwell in one place, being driven hither and yon through want, going about the desert on foot. He has been fighting since the time of Horus; he never conquers, and he does not announce a day of fighting, like a thief whom the community has driven out. . . . Do not worry about him, for the Asiatic is a crocodile on his riverbank; he snatches a lonely serf, but he will never rob in the vicinity of a populous town ('The Teaching for Merikare,' in W. K. Simpson, *The Literature of Ancient Egypt*, pp. 187f.).

These 'wretched Asiatics' are probably to be related to the people called the Martu by the Sumerians and Amurru ('westerners') by the Akkadians and Amorites by most scholars of today. In the last centuries of the third millennium, they appear to have spread from their home in Syria and settled throughout the Fertile Crescent from Ur in the southeast to Palestine and Egypt in the southwest. They were opposed at Ur in the time of Ur's third dynasty (*c.* 2060–1950 BC); *c.* 1970 BC Ammenemes I of Dynasty XII campaigned vigorously against the Asiatics and built 'the walls of the Ruler, made to repel the Satyu [Asiatics] and to crush the Sandfarers'. From now on Egypt began to reassert her presence in Palestine, enjoying diplomatic and commercial relations, if not complete political domination. The story of Sinuhe shows how much contact there was. Sinuhe was rescued from death by an Asiatic chief who had been to Egypt. Another chief told Sinuhe, 'You will be well with me, for you will hear the speech of Egypt,' and asked after news from Egypt. Egyptian jewellery has been found at Byblos, and statues of Egyptian officials at Ras Shamra and Megiddo. At Jericho was found the seal of a scribe of the vizier which may come from this period.

This brings us to Jericho's position in the land at the end of the Intermediate EB–MB age. Here the evidence of the 'Execration texts', negative though it is, may be important. These texts are red pottery bowls, or limestone figures of local princes represented as prisoners, bearing names of persons or places in Egyptian hieratic script, dating from the nineteenth century BC. These sherds or figurines were ritually broken to express the idea of Egypt's victory over or domination of potential or real foreign enemies. A number of persons and places from Palestine are included, the personal names all being Semitic names, probably of people whose ancestors entered Palestine in the Intermediate EB–MB period. Places such as Jerusalem and Ashkelon appear, but noticeably absent are Megiddo, Ugarit and other major towns – perhaps because these were towns where Egyptian influence was strong and which could be relied upon to support Egypt.

Jericho does not appear – either because it was a place of little importance, or because it was safely pro-Egyptian, complete, perhaps, with minor Egyptian officials, as the seal mentioned above might indicate. But this brings us to the beginning of the MB I period, when Egypt is reasserting her power in Syria and Palestine, and the cities of Palestine are on their way to the urban revival of MB II.

Jericho in the Middle Bronze Age

The beginning of the MB age is notoriously difficult to date. As we have seen, American scholars tend to use MB I to denote the later part of what British scholars call Intermediate EB–MB. This period is dated by Kenyon c. 2300–1900 BC, her MB I period thus beginning c. 1900 and lasting only a comparatively short while until c. 1850. Some scholars would push the beginning of this period back towards 2000, but in any case it represents the beginning of the re-emergence of urban life in Palestine after the somewhat 'dark age' of Intermediate EB–MB, and it is roughly contemporary with the renewal of Egyptian interest in Palestine which we have already sketched. It is generally agreed, however, first, that the material culture of MB I did not arise wholly from the preceding Intermediate EB–MB period, but shows unmistakable signs of the arrival of new groups of Amorites, already urbanised by contact with Byblos and the towns of southern Syria, and, secondly, that the restoration of urban life in Palestine was a slow process which did not really get under way until the nineteenth century BC. Buildings begin to appear at a number of sites. At Jericho, on the east side of the mound, a mud-brick tomb of this period was found, and also two individual graves. No MB I tombs were found in the cemetery areas north and west of the tell, and there is no evidence of MB I building on the tell, but this may be partly because there were very few places on the tell, thanks to erosion, where MB I levels could be explored. It may also be because the period was a short one. There is certainly less indication of life and occupation at MB I Jericho than there is for the preceding period. If the newcomers spread through Palestine from the north, however, Jericho might not be expected to be the first city to show signs of their presence, and it may have taken some time for Jericho to rise again as a city.

When she did, it was as one of a large number of thriving Palestinian cities. Excavation shows that most of them, like Jericho, show few signs of life in MB I, but that there are signs of expansion and improvement of defences towards the end of the 18th century BC when at Jericho, Tell ed-Duweir, Gezer, Hazor, Tell el-Farᶜah, and Shechem large banks or ramparts of earth, covered with plaster, are built in front of the town walls. This perhaps ushered in the final impressive century of the MB II period (known to many archaeologists as MB IIC), which ended in the early 16th century BC with the re-establishment of Egyptian control of Palestine by the eighteenth dynasty. The success and prosperity of the MB II period was due in part to the failure of the pharaohs of Dynasties XIII and XIV in Egypt in the 18th century BC to maintain the standards and power of the Middle Kingdom dynasties XI and XII. Under Dynasty XIII Semitic foreigners became influential in Egypt – some scholars have seen here the background of the Joseph story – and by Dynasty XV the rulers of Egypt were Amorites, ruling Egypt for the next century from the Delta region. This so-called 'Hyksos' age is roughly contemporary with the final stage of MB II in Palestine, and in fact represents an extension into Egypt of the MB civilisation of Palestine. Towards the end of the 17th century BC, however, the Egyptian kings of Dynasty XVII, ruling from Thebes 500 miles up the Nile, began a war of liberation. Under Ahmosis, the first Pharaoh of Dynasty XVIII, the foreign rulers were driven out of the Delta. The destruction in Palestine towards the middle of the 16th century BC of such sites as Jericho, Tell Beit Mirsim, Shechem, Megiddo and Hazor has often been related to the decline in power of these Amorite rulers and their expulsion from Egypt, and these destructions conveniently mark the conventional end of the MB age in Palestine.

Excavation has revealed much of MB II Jericho (c. 1800–1550 BC). In the 18th century a town existed on the tell, complete with a mud-brick wall about 2 m thick, similar in type to the earlier EB walls. Evidence of this wall, and of a gateway probably giving access to the spring, was found on the southeast side of the tell (south of squares H III and VI) and also at the northwest corner of the tell. Probably the wall followed the line of the earlier EB wall round the mound. Kenyon found evidence of three rebuilds of this early MB II wall. About the end of the 18th century the city was extended and completely new, larger defences were built. That the city was extended is clear from the fact that the last MB building phases, a collection of shops and business premises on the southeast slopes of the mound, were built over the top of the first MB wall and ran out towards the east. Part of the new defence system was traced by Sellin and Watzinger. At the northeast corner of the tell this wall swung further out to the east than its predecessors, and originally must have enclosed ground on the east side of the tell now occupied by the road and the pools filled by the spring. This new defence system may have been partly designed to enclose the water supply within the walls of the town. If so, a new problem was created, for the water would have to flow out through the walls somewhere, and this would create a weak point in the defences. No traces of any conduit can now be seen. The wall traced

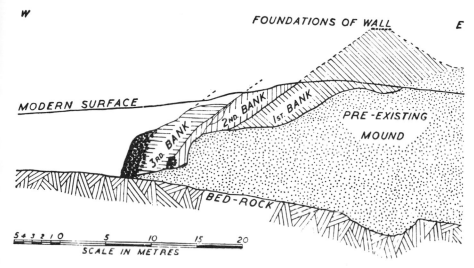

Figure 16   Reconstructed section of Middle Bronze II rampart at Jericho.

by Sellin and Watzinger (originally dated by them to the Iron age) turned out to be the revetment supporting the bottom of a large earthen bank faced by a thick, hard lime-plastered surface designed to hold the earth in place, and surmounted by a large mud-brick curtain wall. The mound was earthed up in stages, each stage being held in place by a layer of plaster, and it reached a height of 14 m above the external ground level. The wall itself was set back 20 m from the foot of the slope, the angle of which was 35°. Inside the wall, as is clear from the northwest corner of the tell where the slope has survived to its full height, there was a reverse slope running down about 4 m into the city.

The clearest evidence for this great rampart comes from the west side of the tell, and can be seen best in the section of Trench I. A simplified section is shown in Figure 16. Above the surface left by the Intermediate EB–MB period which sloped gradually to the west, a soil fill was deposited, finished off with a thick plaster surface. Above this was deposited another fill, which was given a slightly steeper slope but a thinner plaster surface. At its bottom is the remains of a revetting wall of bricks. In front of this was the third stage, consisting of a large fill held in place with a solid revetting wall built on the bedrock, which had been cleared for the purpose. The plaster of this phase, however, did not survive at this point of the tell (Trench I), though as we have seen it survived at the northwest corner. The evidence of Trench

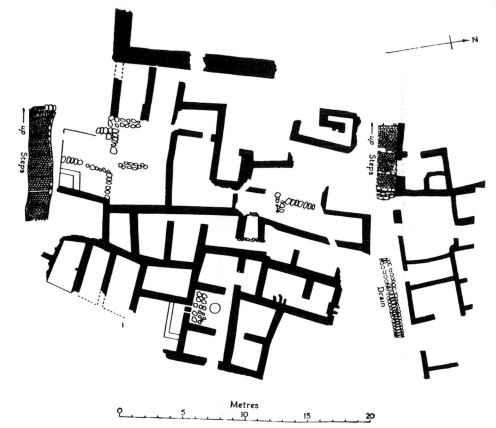

Figure 17   Plan of Middle Bronze II houses on the east slope of Tell es-Sultan.

I thus shows that there were at least two rebuildings of the plastered slope at this point.

Ramparts of this or similar type have been found at a number of MB II sites in Egypt, Palestine and Syria. Kenyon suggested that this means of defence was introduced by the 'Hyksos', whom she explains as a military aristocracy deriving from Hurrian and Habiru peoples settling in Palestine at this time. The Hurrians began settling in upper Mesopotamia in the early centuries of the second millennium BC; by the 15th century their state Mitanni was the dominant power in Mesopotamia and north Syria. As de Vaux points out, however, Hurrian presence in Palestine dates only from the 15th century, and this is too late for the Hurrians to have any part in the introduction of new defences in the late 18th century MB II Palestine. The Habiru, to judge from the known personal names, may be partly Hurrian in origin, but by the mid-second millennium they appear as independent

Plate 14   A stepped street of the Middle Bronze Age, Tell es-Sultan.

fringe-groups who take employment and settle where they can, appearing as slaves, workmen, and mercenary soldiers. It has often been suggested that the Habiru were the forerunners of the biblical Hebrews. That there is a connection is generally agreed, but the total identity of Habiru and Hebrews is generally denied. Probably the Habiru were one constituent part of what was to become the people of Israel.

The evidence linking the introduction of the plaster-faced ramparts with a military aristocracy composed of Hurrians and Habiru is not compelling, and it is simpler to suppose that the ramparts belong to the Canaanite/Amorite Middle Bronze period at the height of its development, when its influence extended even into Egypt. The introduction of these ramparts does not necessarily indicate the arrival of a new people, and Kenyon herself emphasised that there was no evidence of a new culture in the towns of this period. It has often been suggested that this new type of defence was invented as an answer to chariot warfare, or the use of the bow and arrow (whose range is greater than that of a spear), or the use of battering rams. The more likely explanation has been advanced that these ramparts originated in the earlier custom of consolidating and regularising and augmenting in the interests of security the natural slopes of the tells. These ramparts are a natural development which evolved as the tells grew in height. The ramparts may also have served (as was recently suggested to me by a construction engineer) to support the weight of the huge town wall on top of them and to prevent their being undermined by erosion of the slopes by the winter rains.

Within these plastered ramparts, a certain amount of the final stages of MB Jericho has survived. Over most of the tell, the evidence is missing, probably destroyed by erosion. No occupation levels are visible in Trench I on the west. On the southeast, however, building levels run out east across the line of the earlier MB wall (Figure 17). Garstang here found rooms containing jars of carbonised grain, and he described them as storerooms belonging to a nearby palace. Kenyon, however, showed that these rooms were earlier than the 'palace', and that the area was one of private houses, shops and business premises. Two parallel cobbled streets about 2 m wide rise up the hill in a series of long steps (Plate 14). Small one-roomed shops opened off them. These buildings had an upper storey which might serve as living accommodation or sometimes as manufacturing premises. A large number of loom weights in one place, and 52 saddle querns and a collection of rubbing stones in another, probably witness to weaving and cornmilling. This area was a new quarter, conveniently sited near the spring; it began life when the MB city was extended towards the end of the 18th century, and lasted for about another 100–150 years.

Plate 15   Middle Bronze Age II Tomb H18.

The best evidence for the life of MB Jericho has come from the MB II tombs rather than from the tell. Garstang excavated 22, and Kenyon 51 out of the 80 she discovered. Of these 51, only 9 were first dug in the MB age, the rest being reused EB shaft tombs. Unlike the Intermediate EB–MB tombs, these MB tombs contained multiple burials, usually any number up to 20, though one tomb held 45. Earlier burials would be pushed to the back or partly ejected to make room for later ones. From the tombs excavated, a combination of skull-counting and estimation suggests an 'ascertainable number' of burials at 1150. If one doubles this to allow for undiscovered tombs, the resultant total is hardly enough to account for the MB II population of Jericho from *c*. 1800–1550 BC. These tombs probably belonged to the leading or wealthier families, poorer people being buried elsewhere. The practice of multiple burial may not be so much a totally new practice as the extension and development of the Intermediate EB–MB practice. These tombs with multiple burials are normally the result of successive interments over a period of time; however, there are six examples of multiple simultaneous burials which appear to contain family groups, the head of the family being marked out by being placed on a mud-brick platform or a bed. Tomb P19 (now reconstructed in the Room of Ancient Palestine in the British Museum) is intriguing; it contains the disarranged skeleton of a

Plate 16   Bone inlay from toilet box, Middle Bronze Age II Tomb H22.

young woman, and a further six skeletons (2 men, 3 women, and a boy) apparently killed by a blow on the head. The two men had their hands cut off. In another tomb, each skeleton had at least one forearm removed; the reason is unknown.

Something of the standard of living in MB Jericho can be gauged from the evidence of the tombs, for by some natural process organic material left in the tombs over 3500 years ago – leather, wood, animal meat, human skin and hair – was partially preserved until its excavation between 1952–59. F. E. Zeuner (*Palestine Exploration Quarterly* (1955), pp. 118–128) noted that there was a high humidity content in the tombs, in which therefore rapid decomposition could be expected and had at first taken place. Wood had rotted, and had been attacked by insects. But the rot and the insects had apparently ceased work before the wood was totally consumed. Zeuner suggested that the rot was stopped either by the self-generation in a confined space of carbon-dioxide and methane from the decomposition of organic matter under alkaline conditions (the methane might have checked the decay), or by the intrusion of natural gas through faults in the limestone caused by earth movements.

To judge from the contents of the tombs, the MB Jerichoans could live

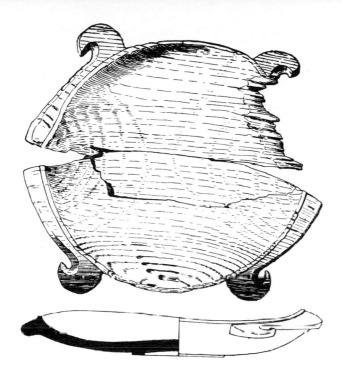

Figure 18 Wooden bowl from Middle Bronze Jericho, Tomb H6.

in reasonable comfort, but not opulently. Only five tombs had gold or items
of particular value – some gold-mounted scarabs, and a gold band which
had probably adorned a cylindrical box. A wealthy man might have a bed
and a stool; the less wealthy probably slept as they were buried on mats.
They wore woven garments, held in place by a toggle-pin fixed below the
left shoulder. They used wooden combs; a basket in one tomb appeared to
contain a wig, dyed with henna. Other small personal items included ala-
baster bowls and jars for oil or scent, wooden boxes inlaid with bone decoration (Plate 16), oval wooden bowls with four handles carved in ram's
head form (Figure 18), and beads and scarabs. Clearly there was a good deal
of carpentry at MB Jericho. Beds and stools (with woven tops) have been
mentioned; tables were made with three legs (two legs at one end, one at the
other) in order to stand steady on an uneven floor. Various local timbers
were used – tamarisk, willow, wild cherry, hornbeam and thorn. Date palm
leaves were used to weave bags and matting. Meat and drink was left in the
tombs for the dead; fruit found in the tombs includes pomegranates, dates
and grapes.

The pottery of MB II Jericho is among the most handsome of the whole
Palestinian repertoire. The shapes are generally graceful, varied, and more

Plate 17 Middle Bronze Age II pottery from Jericho Tomb P19.

accurately made than previously. Kenyon distinguished five successive phases of pottery from the tombs. In the earliest, globular bowls and piriform juglets predominate; in the second, flaring carinated bowls and pedestal vases appear. In phase 3, cylindrical juglets appear and the deeper globular bowls become rarer. In phase 4, the cylindrical juglets have virtually taken over from the button-based variety, and faience bottles and ornamental toggle-pins appear. In the last phase, the repertoire includes the flaring carinate bowls, wide bowls with upright walls, pedestal vases, cylindrical juglets, faience bottles and toggle-pins. The globular bowls and piriform juglets have completely disappeared. The majority of the tombs fall into phases 2 and 3, which may mean that these phases represent a longer, or a wealthier period than the other phases. The great difficulty, however, lies in correlating these pottery phases with the history of the tell. Kenyon notes that the pottery belonging to the period of the extension of the town eastwards belongs with phase 3 of the tomb pottery; since phase 3 can probably be dated on the evidence of scarabs found in the tombs to the early and middle parts of the 17th century BC (see Figure 19), the extension of the town and the building of the plastered rampart probably belong to the late 18th century. Phase 3 represents the period from which the greatest number of MB tombs have been found, and the 17th century was probably the peak period of MB II Jericho's prosperity.

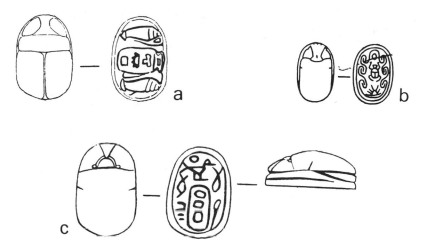

Figure 19 Three scarabs from Middle Bronze Jericho: *a.* bearing the name Khahopepre; *b.* from Tomb 9, bearing the name Kheperkhere, a variant of the pre-nomen of Sesostris II; *c.* scarab of the 'Son of Re Sheshi' class.

The end of MB Jericho was violent, as is shown by the burnt ruins of the final level of MB buildings on the southeast side of the tell. The ruined walls are covered by a layer of burnt debris one metre thick washed down from higher up the slope. This layer shows clearly that the higher buildings were burned, and that a considerable period of erosion followed the destruction of the site. The tombs show that burials ceased in the early sixteenth century BC, and, according to Kenyon, the pottery of the later 16th century and most of the 15th century – in particular, the Bichrome ware and the Cypriot black lustrous ware – is completely missing. The fact of MB Jericho's destruction is clear, the reason for it less so. It has often been suggested that the Egyptians were responsible as they pursued the 'Hyksos' into Palestine after expelling them from Egypt, but there is no evidence that the Egyptians pursued the Asiatic rulers further than Sharuhen. Another suggestion is that the Asiatics displaced from Egypt were themselves responsible for the various destructions in 16th century Palestine. A recent attempt has been made, on the basis of a biblical chronology, to demonstrate that MB Jericho was destroyed not in the 16th but in the 15th century *c.* 1440 BC, by invading Israelites. This involves, among other things, the total redating of the MB age, and of the 'bichrome ware' hitherto generally dated to the 15th–14th centuries, and it solves the problem raised by a 13th century capture of Jericho (when on archaeological evidence a walled city of Jericho did not

Figure 20   Bichrome ware krater from Lachish, Temple I.

exist) by creating the new problem of a 15th century capture of Jericho (when again on the usual interpretation of the archaeological evidence a walled city of Jericho did not exist).

The destruction of cities is not always the work of enemies. Kenyon argued that the death of families in the 'multiple simultaneous burial' tombs was caused by some single catastrophic event shortly before the final destruction of the town (for the tombs were not used again), and suggested disease as the cause. The state of the tombs and the strange phenomenon noted above of the arrested decay of organic objects points to earthquake activity, and the tell shows traces of fire. Plague, earthquake and fire might of themselves have been major factors in bringing about the end of MB Jericho.

It is not easy to date precisely either the end of MB Jericho or the end of the MB age in Palestine. It has recently been argued that there is no real change in Palestine's material culture until after 1500 BC; the dividing point

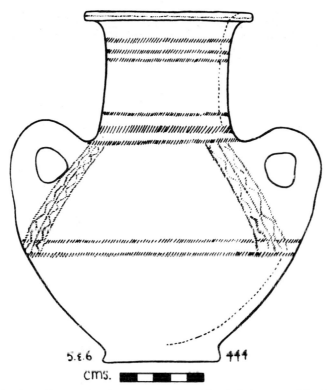

Figure 21   Late Bronze Age jug from Jericho, Tomb 5 (excavated by J. Garstang).

might be the period of Egyptian campaigns in and through Palestine under the Dynasty XVIII Pharaohs Thutmosis I (1508–1494 BC) and Thutmosis II (1486–1436 BC). Thutmosis III is known to have destroyed a number of cities, especially in the north (Megiddo, Taanach, Hazor). But more visible evidence for a dividing line between Middle and Late Bronze comes in the pottery. New types appear, including the 'bichrome ware' with its distinctive decoration (Figure 20). This is painted ware, emanating from the Canaanite coast, using pottery forms drawn from both the Palestinian MB II tradition and also from the Cypriot types. The decoration portrays ibexes, birds and fish in a frieze on the neck and shoulder of the pot. Imported Cypriot pottery is important in this period; common are the white-painted and white-slip wares, and the base-ring ware. Kenyon dates this material to the century or so before c. 1470 BC. The dating is far from precise, but if it is roughly correct, the important point for our purpose is that Jericho, along with other sites of southern and central Palestine (Tell Beit Mirsim, Tell Gezer, Shiloh,

Bethel and Gibeon), does not show any sign of having used the bichrome ware and imported Cypriot pottery. The explanation is not simply that Jericho was a backwater in the Jordan valley which bichrome ware, spreading inland from the coast, failed to reach, for that leaves its failure to reach places like Tell Beit Mirsim unexplained, and in any case it is not just bichrome ware but a whole range of pottery of the period that is missing from Jericho. The obvious explanation is that there was a break in the occupation of the tell after the destruction of the MB II city. This is indicated particularly by the layer of ash washed down from above over the walls of the MB II buildings on the southeastern part of the tell. Burials in the tombs cease; a few vessels from Garstang's tomb 5 (Figure 21) might be attributable to the 15th century, but the evidence is slight and not enough to demonstrate that the city was occupied and active. Kenyon believes that the tell was unoccupied until *c*. 1400 BC.

Jericho in the Late Bronze Age

To the dismay of historians and others interested in the settlement of the early Israelites in their land, the archaeological evidence for Tell es-Sultan in the Late Bronze age is tantalisingly scanty. Garstang had pointed to a double wall on top of the mound, which he believed Joshua had destroyed *c*. 1400 BC, and to evidence both positive and negative from tombs 4, 5 and 13. Positively, the discovery of two royal signet rings buried with their owners and bearing the insignia of Amenophis III (1405–1367 BC), together with pottery from tomb 5 and from the 'palace storerooms' which Garstang dated to the end of the 15th century BC, suggested that there was occupation at Jericho until *c*. 1400. Negatively, Garstang argued that the absence of Mycenaean pottery, the absence of scarabs after the reign of Amenophis III, and the absence of reference to Jericho in the Amarna letters, which give a picture of the political situation in Palestine in the reign of Amenophis IV (1367–1350 BC), all point to the abandonment of Tell es-Sultan in the fourteenth century.

Kenyon, however, has argued for a very different picture of LB Jericho. As we have seen, she demonstrated that the 'double wall' belonged to the EB age and had nothing to do with Joshua. She showed that the tombs excavated by Garstang were MB tombs, though reused in the 14th century; apart from a few vessels in tomb 5 they did not evidence life at Jericho in the 15th century BC. She did, however, produce a small amount of new evidence for the existence of a settlement at Tell es-Sultan during at least part of the LB age. Above the layer of wash from the burnt MB city in

Plate 18   The remains of a Late Bronze Age house and oven on Tell es-Sultan.

square H III, Kenyon found a row of stones which she interpreted as the foundation of a room wall. Associated with it was a small irregular area of floor, on which was a mud oven and a dipper juglet of 14th century BC type, 'the only Late Bronze Age vessel we have found *in situ* on the tell' (Plate 18). Attempts to find further evidence in a neighbouring square were frustrated by the fact that the area had already been excavated by previous expeditions. One might add to Kenyon's evidence a clay tablet discovered by Garstang, 'rather burnt and damaged', bearing a largely obliterated cuneiform inscription which was tentatively dated to the 14th century BC.

Kenyon argues that this evidence, such as it is, indicates the existence of a small settlement on the tell between *c.* 1400 and 1325 BC, or even slightly after 1300. But there is no sign of a city wall belonging specifically to this period. It has sometimes been suggested that the inhabitants used the remains of the walls of the MB city. If they did, however, there are no signs of the debris of LB occupation against those walls. If the evidence for the LB occupation of the tell has been eroded away by wind and rain (as has often been suggested), traces of this erosion would have been found in the wash at the foot of the tell. But while this can be found for the MB period, it cannot be found for the LB period. Recent re-investigation of the work of Sellin and Watzinger and of Garstang by M. and H. Weippert (*Zeitschrift des Deutschen Palästina-Vereins* 92 (1976), pp. 105–148) has suggested that LB Jericho was probably limited in area to the region of the 'Middle Building'. (This building was discovered in the southeastern area of the tell by Garstang and so named because it lay above the MB levels and below the Iron Age 'Hilani' building; Kenyon dated it to the 14th century.) There was evidence of LB occupation beneath the 'Hilani' building, but not underneath a neighbouring Iron Age building. Kenyon similarly notes that while there is evidence for an LB house in square H III, in a neighbouring square the Iron Age filling 'went right down into the deep gullies cutting into the MBA levels. Evidence was thus produced of the eroded state of the tell at the time when the Iron Age settlement was established.'

With such limited evidence, it is hard to reconstruct the history or the life of Jericho in the 16th–13th centuries BC. The archaeological evidence does not give us any very precise dating, and it does not help us identify the 14th century settlers on the tell. It is difficult to relate the archaeological evidence and the biblical narrative of the capture of Jericho by Joshua, as we shall see in the next chapter. Jericho is not mentioned in the Egyptian records, either in the description of Thutmosis III's campaign in the 15th century or in the Amarna letters in the 14th century. Thutmosis III seems to have ignored and bypassed southeast Palestine, and in the Amarna age, if Jericho was occupied, the writers of the Amarna letters do not seem to have taken any notice of it. In this period, according to Y. Aharoni, 'the centres of Canaanite population came more and more to be concentrated along the main branches of the *Via Maris*, while the interior regions of the country were less heavily settled'. The Egyptian administration was based upon Gaza, from which it controlled the routes north to Syria. Jericho was not of much political importance in the LB age.

For further reference

J. B. Hennessy, *The Foreign Relations of Palestine during the Early Bronze Age*, Quaritch, London, 1967.
K. M. Kenyon, *The Archaeology of the Holy Land*, 4th edn., Benn, London; Norton, New York, 1979.
K. M. Kenyon, *Jericho I*, *Jericho II*, British School of Archaeology in Jerusalem, London, 1960, 1965.
R. de Vaux, *The Early History of Israel*, 2 volumes, Darton, Longman and Todd, London, 1978.
J. Bright, *A History of Israel*, 2nd edn., S.C.M. Press, London, 1972.
Y. Aharoni, *The Land of the Bible*, 2nd edn., Burns & Oates, London, 1979.

6

Israelite Jericho

Most people think of Jericho first of all as a biblical city. The story of its capture by Joshua suggests at once that Jericho existed before the Israelites came on the scene, and the excavations of the last century have progressively revealed that Jericho's history stretches back a very long way indeed. Our knowledge of this history depends entirely on the archaeologists until we reach mention of Jericho in the Old Testament. Archaeological evidence for the Jericho of the Old Testament period exists, but the Old Testament references to Jericho add a new dimension to the evidence, and much of this chapter will necessarily be devoted to interpreting the literary evidence. Just as the soil of an ancient tell contains many strata, each the deposit of some human activity, which need separating and interpreting, so the Old Testament, the deposit of a millennium's literary activity, contains many strata, which need separating and interpreting. The different strata, however, of the two lines of evidence, archaeological and literary, are not always easy to relate to each other. Jericho is a classic example of this problem, for reasons which may become clearer as this chapter proceeds.

It is far from certain in what year (or even in which century) Jericho became Israelite. Some scholars suggest the 15th century, some the 13th, and some the 12th. We have already examined the archaeological evidence for LB Jericho, which brings us to the end of the 13th century, and it remains to say something about the archaeological evidence for the Iron Age, from the 12th to the 4th century BC. This has recently been gathered together and assessed by M. and H. Weippert (*Zeitschrift des Deutschen Palästina–Vereins* 92 (1976), pp. 105–148). They argue that the Iron Age pottery discovered on the *Quellhügel* ranges from the 11th to the early 6th century BC, and that the quality of this pottery makes it likely that we are to think of a continuous settlement here throughout this period. The earliest evidence appears to be an Early Iron age (?) fragment of a sieve jar in the foundations of the 'Hilani' building (Figure 23). In this building, perhaps datable to the 10th century by comparison with Building 6000 at Megiddo, were found two small Iron Age I (11th century) jars and a pyxis (a small, squat jar, with two handles rising from the shoulder) of Iron Age IIA–B (10th–9th century).

How long this building lasted is uncertain, for only its foundations were left, somewhat eroded and robbed. It is possible that, as an important public building, it lasted well into the middle of Iron Age Jericho; it is partly covered by walls of Iron Age IIC. Alongside it stood a number of Iron Age houses (ten were identified) (Figure 24). The outer walls were built of mud-brick on a stone foundation, and the inner walls of mud-brick alone, with a mud-plaster covering. The lay-out of three houses has been established, and it corresponds to that of other known Iron Age Israelite houses. The pottery found in these houses ranges from Iron Age I–IIC; thus the last occupation of the houses may be dated to the 8th–7th centuries BC.

Further evidence of Iron Age II settlement of the tell was found at the foot of the tell on the west. At the bottom end of Kenyon's Trench I, an area covered with silt and wash brought down by erosion had been levelled. Occupation began with a fireplace; there followed a building which, after two occupation levels, was burnt. A substantial building of three or four rooms followed; it too was burnt. After further erosion and levelling, a final building – perhaps sheep and cattle pens – was attempted. This in turn was covered with silt containing sherds of Iron Age II. The area thus evidences domestic settlement at the foot of the tell in the middle of the Iron Age. Its position may suggest that the city was without walls at the time, or perhaps that (as happened elsewhere) in times of comparative security houses could be built outside the walls. The final layer of silt perhaps accumulated after the end of Iron Age Jericho when Iron Age pottery was lying on the surface of the slopes of the tell.

The evidence for Iron Age tombs is also scanty. Sellin and Watzinger found an Iron Age II tomb dug into the 'Hilani' building. Garstang found two graves, one apparently from the 11th–10th centuries BC, west of the tell. Kenyon found a 10th century grave north of the tell, and two 8th–7th century graves southwest of the tell. An ivory bull's head (originally attached to a piece of furniture) found by Garstang in 1931 should perhaps also be attributed to the Iron Age, rather than to the MB age. Sellin and Watzinger found one royal stamped jar-handle, of the two-winged variety, from the late 8th or 7th century BC. The inscription, only partly legible, probably read, 'for the king. Socoh'. Such stamps are well known, and probably denote either produce from the royal estates or local produce delivered to the crown by way of taxation.

All this does not amount to very much, and there is even less evidence for the final stages of the Iron Age at Tell es-Sultan. Sellin and Watzinger found pottery and houses from the Persian period at the northern end of the tell. There is a certain amount of epigraphic evidence, including a number of 5th–4th century jar handles stamped *yhd* (i.e. the Persian province of Judah)

Figure 22   Iron Age pottery from Jericho (excavated by Sellin and Watzinger).

and *mṣh* (probably a place-name) (Plate 19). One such seal impression perhaps reads *belonging to Hagar*/(daughter of) *Uriah* or *Yehud/Uriah*, Uriah probably being an important official. Another impression on a jar shows a male figure grasping a lion (?) by the tail. The man wears his hair in a bun, and has a quiver or a wing on his shoulder. Above is a solar disc (with a seated figure on it?). The style is perhaps Persian. Under Persian administration, Tell es-Sultan was probably occupied, and may have been used as an administrative centre of the province of Judah.

This limited archaeological evidence for Iron Age Jericho by itself gives a poor picture of Israelite Jericho. It gives us no personal names (except perhaps one on a post-exilic seal impression), no fixed dates, no major events. For these we have to examine the literary evidence, which needs careful evaluation and interpretation. We need to know the writers' sources and how they handle them, and to allow for their theological, philosophical or political aims in writing, and to assess the authenticity of the texts. This applies as much to writings from ancient Israel as it does to documents from ancient Greece and Rome or medieval Europe.

The only account of the Israelite capture of Jericho after the Exodus from Egypt has been handed down to us in a book called *Joshua*. It is a book not by Joshua but about Joshua, and was written as part of a lengthy history ('the Deuteronomistic history work') spanning the period from the end of Moses' career to the end of the kingdom of Judah in 587 BC. When this work was compiled, the deeds of Joshua were already six or seven hundred years past. The questions for the historian of Jericho are, 'What source or sources was the historian using in Joshua chapters 2 and 6, and what is their value?' and, 'Was the purpose of the original author (and of the Deuteronomistic historian) to describe for the satisfaction of the modern enquirer what happened at Jericho, or was it something different?'

The account of Joshua 2 is mainly devoted to the story of the sending of the two men from the Israelite camp 'to view the land, especially Jericho'. They do not in fact view the land, but they do visit Jericho, where all the action takes place. Rahab hides them, misdirects the local security forces, tells the spies of the Jerichoans' poor morale, and asks that her family will be spared when Jericho falls. The spies promise this, depart through Rahab's window in the town wall to the hills to wait till the hue and cry is off before returning to Joshua to report that 'Truly the Lord has given all the land into our hands; and moreover, all the inhabitants of the land are fainthearted because of us'.

These words, and the words assigned to Rahab in Joshua 2:11, reveal one of the story-teller's main interests. He is trying to demonstrate that from the start the conquest of Canaan was an act of the Lord, not of the Israelites.

102

Plate 19
Three stamped jar-handles
from Tell es-Sultan,
reading *mṣh*, *yh yh*.

This is a holy war, in which the Lord fights on Israel's side and fills the enemy with panic. Another feature of the story is that it is intended to explain how it was that the well-known Canaanite family of Rahab was found living in Jericho in the writer's day (cf. Josh. 6:25), in spite of the Deuteronomic law that all Canaanites should be exterminated (cf. Deut. 20:16f.). Third, it is worth noticing that the motif of the sending of spies prior to the invasion of Canaan is a common one (as can be seen from Num. 13–14; 21:32; Deut. 1:22; Josh. 7:2f.; Judg. 18:2ff.). It is almost a necessary preliminary to any story about invading and capturing the land. (Other theological motifs may also be at work; for example, the scarlet cord placed in the window as a sign that Rahab's house is to be spared has been seen by some as a parallel to the blood painted on the lintels at the first passover to show that the inhabitants were to be spared.) Joshua 2 in fact tells us very little about the military aspects of the capture of Jericho. The spies' reconnaissance brings no recorded information about Jericho's military strength; it serves mainly to effect the preservation of Rahab's family and to underline the divine support for the Israelites.

The next three chapters of Joshua describe how the Israelites crossed the Jordan, set up twelve stones from the river in the sanctuary of Gilgal, circumcised themselves and kept the passover. The narrator is clearly interested mainly in the cultic (not military) activities of the Israelites at this point; the ark of the covenant occupies a prominent place in the story of the river crossing, which is followed by a series of specifically cultic actions. The narrative returns to the story of Jericho in Joshua 5:13ff.,

> When Joshua was by Jericho, he lifted up his eyes and looked, and behold, a man stood before him with his drawn sword in his hand; and Joshua went to him and said to him, 'Are you for us, or for our adversaries?' And he said, 'No; but as a commander of the army of the LORD I have now come.'

The point of this is that the coming struggle for Jericho is going to be led by the angelic 'commander of the Lord's army'. The historian is saying plainly that the Lord is directing this war (cf. Josh. 6:2). The story of the capture of Jericho now follows, and though it begins like any siege (Josh. 6:1), the subsequent activity sounds more like a liturgical act. The picture is not that of a siege but of a ceremonial procession, the participants following liturgical directions. The basic story (with some confusion of detail, particularly in the matter of the sequence of shoutings and trumpet sounds) describes the processional encircling of the city with ritual trumpet blowings and shouts, with the ark and its attendants, in a festival of seven days. The religious, liturgical aspect is emphasised throughout, and the end of the

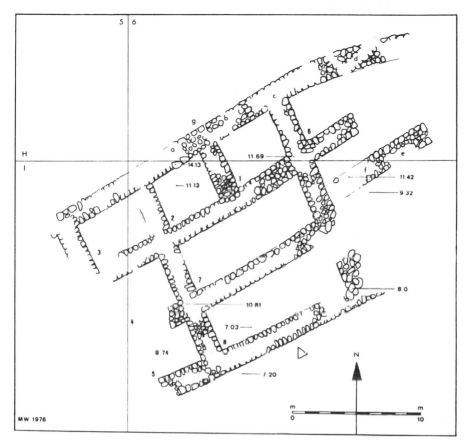

Figure 23 The 'Hilani' building on the *Quellhugel* at Jericho.

matter is that Jericho is to be 'totally devoted to the LORD for destruction'
(Josh. 6:17). The Israelites may keep none of the spoil; 'but all the silver
and gold, and vessels of bronze and iron, are sacred to the LORD; they shall
go into the treasury of the LORD'. The reference here is probably to the
temple treasury at Jerusalem, and betrays the fact that this account belongs
to a period when the Israelites celebrate the event in a temple or sanctuary,
and, further, to a period when what is remembered is not the actual event
but the liturgical reenactment of that event.

The Deuteronomistic historian is using this story for one other purpose.
According to Joshua 6:26,

> Joshua laid an oath on them at that time, saying, 'Cursed before the LORD
> be the man that rises up and rebuilds this city, Jericho.
>   At the cost of his first-born shall he lay its foundation,
>   and at the cost of his youngest son shall he set up its gates.'

The historian has in mind an event which he will describe in due course (1 Kings 16:34), the building of Jericho by Hiel of Bethel. The historian mentions it here because he wishes to explain the circumstances of Hiel's rebuilding of the ruined city by reference to the destruction of Jericho in the time of Joshua. He gives Joshua's curse on would-be rebuilders as the explanation of what happened to Hiel's sons.

In the light of this, how should we assess the historical value of Joshua 2 and 6 for our history of ancient Jericho? These chapters do not attempt to give a factual description of the physical events of a siege and sacking of a city. They do not set the event against the larger political context, and they do not date it by reference to other contemporary events. The narrative reflects the standardised traditions of 'the wars of the Lord' (Num. 21:14) on behalf of Israel. It reflects the liturgical activities of the Israelites, perhaps from the time of the monarchy. But the ceremony of encirclement described in Joshua 6:3 might derive, not from ceremonies at the Jerusalem temple, but from the shrine of Gilgal. The very name Gilgal carries with it the idea of a circle, and is usually connected with a circle of stones not far from Jericho (cf. Josh. 4:19; 5:10). It has often been pointed out that Joshua 2–11 is largely concerned with traditions about the region in which the tribe of Benjamin settled, traditions which were perhaps preserved and celebrated at the sanctuary of Gilgal. If so, the basis of the account in Joshua 6 might be a liturgical rite practised at Gilgal, reenacting the Benjaminite capture of the nearby town of Jericho, in the late twelfth or eleventh century BC, a small place, whose broken down MB walls, however, were still visible reminders of her past glory. But this is speculation. Our literary sources show that the historians drew on knowledge of a ruined Jericho which was rebuilt in monarchic times, and on a liturgical tradition of a conquest of Jericho.

One other important factor contributed to the Deuteronomistic historian's presentation of the story. He was working with the conception that Canaan was conquered by the movement of all Israel invading from Transjordan. Once this idea arose (and it took some time – the evidence suggests that the Israelite conquest and settlement of Canaan took place piecemeal, from different directions, over a lengthy period), it was inevitable that Jericho, placed as it was by an important ford of the Jordan, should have become the first and most important of all the captured cities, and a symbol of the conquest. If, as is highly likely, the ruined walls of MB Jericho were still visible in the monarchic age, it would be natural to explain these by reference to the Israelite conquest of Canaan. The Deuteronomistic historian underlined the importance of the event by describing it in terms drawn from the tradition of 'the wars of the Lord' and set it, together with accounts of other

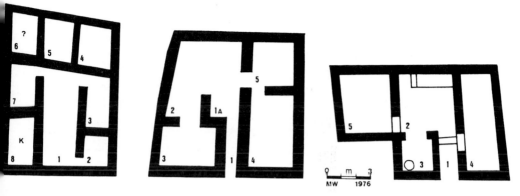

Figure 24   Plans of Iron Age IIC houses at Tell es-Sultan.

such fundamental episodes of Israel's origins as the original circumcision of the Israelites and the first passover held on the soil of Canaan at the beginning of his great work about the history of Israel on her new-found land.

The nature of Israel's recollection of the event at Jericho makes it impossible for the modern historian to relate with any confidence the biblical account and the archaeological evidence of the destruction of Jericho. It is impossible to discover precisely what event underlies the account of Joshua 6. If we make the dubious assumption of an all-Israelite campaign across the Jordan from the east, and date it with many scholars in the late 13th century, we have to meet the archaeological evidence that Jericho hardly existed at the time. A similar problem meets us if we date the event to the 15th century. It may make better sense to think of the capture of Jericho as a comparatively small event of the settlement of the Benjaminites in the land in the 12th or 11th century, when there was nothing much to offer resistance at Jericho. In this case, the Deuteronomistic historian, writing several centuries later, will have enlarged on the Benjaminite tradition in the interests of his major history of Israel. At all events, the solution to the problem is more likely to be found in the correct evaluation of the literary evidence than in further excavation of Tell es-Sultan.

The connection of Jericho with the tribe of Benjamin is made clear in the boundary description of Joshua 18:11–20. Similar boundary descriptions exist for the other northern tribes, and as such descriptions became steadily less relevant with the establishment and success of the kingdoms of Judah and Israel, they probably refer accurately enough to the period when the tribes held their own autonomous territories, in the period before David (i.e. pre-1000 BC). According to the Benjaminite boundary description, the northern boundary of Benjamin 'goes up to the shoulder north of Jericho, then up through the hill country westward' (Josh. 18:12; compare the description of the southern boundary of Ephraim, Josh. 16:1). The southern boundary of Benjamin 'ends at the northern bay of the Salt Sea, at the south end of the Jordan' (Josh. 18:19). The Benjaminite boundaries, then, ran either side of Jericho, the territory tapering off towards the Jordan. Jericho is mentioned in connection with the northern border; Jericho was nearer the northern border than the southern. That Jericho was mentioned at all shows that it was known when the list was made. Jericho, that is, was a Benjaminite town in the late pre-monarchic period; the archaeological evidence suggests that it was a small place. (The Benjaminite city list, however, in Joshua 18:21–27, was probably compiled in the 9th or even 7th century BC and is not evidence for pre-monarchic Jericho.)

Judges 3:12–30 gives an account of an attack in this early period by the Moabites (aided by Amalekites and Ammonites) westward across the Jordan into Benjaminite territory. Judges 3:13 says that they captured 'the city of palm trees' (by which the Deuteronomistic author or editor probably means Jericho; cf. Deut. 34:1,3; 2 Chron. 28:15) and held it, apparently for 18 years, until a Benjaminite hero named Ehud used the opportunity presented by the annual offering of tribute to assassinate Eglon, the king of Moab, as he sat in his cool roof-chamber. It is often assumed (and perhaps the Deuteronomistic historian assumed) that this event took place in Jericho, but this assumption makes the geographical details of verse 19 very hard to follow. If, however, the tribute was paid at the royal palace somewhere in Moab, after which Ehud returned to Benjaminite territory, a turn-about at Gilgal (verse 19) just across the Jordan inside Benjaminite territory, where the accompanying party of bearers and others might be left, and the return of Ehud alone into Moab would make good sense. After the assassination, Ehud fled back into Benjaminite territory via Gilgal and Seirah (verse 26) – the uninhabited chalk marl at the foot of the hills – to organise a force to prevent the pursuing Moabites from crossing the Jordan to take vengeance. The main story does not refer to Jericho at all; it was not a particularly important place, and played no real part in the action.

We hear nothing of Jericho in the reign of Saul (though we hear enough of nearby Gilgal), and this perhaps confirms that Jericho was not a particularly important place at this period. But when David came to the throne and ruled over both Israel and Judah from the new capital of Jerusalem, the situation changed. David had first diplomatic relationships and then direct military confrontation with the kingdom of the Ammonites, ruled from Rabbath-Ammon (modern Amman) east of the Jordan. The importance of Jericho as a border town and staging post on the route was increased by the opening up of political communications between the east and west banks of the Jordan (cf., e.g., 1 Sam. 22:3f.). When David's ambassadors went to Rabbath-Ammon on the occasion of the death of the Ammonite king, they were met by suspicion and maltreated,

> But the princes of the Ammonites said to Hanun their lord, 'Do you think because David has sent comforters to you, that he is honouring your father? Has not David sent his servants to you to search the city, and to spy it out, and to overthrow it?' So Hanun took David's servants, and shaved off half the beard of each, and cut off their garments in the middle, at their hips, and sent them away. When it was told David, he sent to meet them, for the men were greatly ashamed. And the king said, 'Remain at Jericho until your beards have grown, and then return' (2 Sam. 10:3–5).

Jericho, however, is still not much more than a small village, almost certainly without defensive walls. The campaign of Shishak (1 Kings 14:25 = Shoshenq I, c. 945–924 BC) in the fifth year of Rehoboam of Judah seems to have ignored the Jericho region. We next hear of Jericho in the time of Ahab, king of Israel (c. 875–853 BC):

> Hiel of Bethel built Jericho; he laid its foundations at the cost of Ahiram his firstborn, and set up its gates at the cost of his youngest son Segub, according to the word of the LORD, which he spoke by Joshua the son of Nun (1 Kings 16:34).

This interesting passage shows, first, that Jericho was now regarded as part of the northern kingdom of Israel and came under the authority of the king of Israel. Jericho was built by a man from Bethel, a Benjaminite town and important northern sanctuary (Josh. 18:22; 1 Kings 12:29). Hiel 'built' Jericho with 'foundations' and 'gates'; that is, he probably turned an open village into something with better defences. Kenyon discovered some buildings which might belong to this period, but no sign of Hiel's gates has been discovered. If there was a wall, it was probably of mud-brick, or perhaps of wood, long since disintegrated. Given the political circumstances of the time, the reason for the fortification of Jericho is clear. It was in Ahab's time that Moab, southeast of Jericho across the Jordan and originally subjected in David's time (2 Sam. 8:2), rebelled against Israelite rule, as we know from the inscribed pillar (the 'Moabite stone') set up *c.* 830 BC by Mesha, king of Moab,

> Omri, king of Israel, had oppressed Moab many days, for Chemosh was angry with his land. His son succeeded him, and he too said, I will oppress Moab. In my days he said it; but I saw my desire upon him and his house, and Israel perished utterly for ever.

2 Kings 1:1 and 2 Kings 3 refer to campaigns against Moab after Ahab's death. In fortifying Jericho, Ahab was preparing his eastern border against possible Moabite invasion, or as a base camp for Israelite campaigns in Moab. Jericho once again prospered, in effect subsidised by the Israelite government. Why Jericho was founded 'at the cost of' two of Hiel's sons is not clear. Some think a foundation sacrifice is meant, others that the natural death of Hiel's sons was interpreted as fulfilling Joshua's curse on attempts to refound Jericho (Josh. 6:26). A recent suggestion connects the event with the comment on Jericho made to Elisha in 2 Kings 2:19ff., 'the water is bad and the land unfruitful', the reference here being to human miscarriage. Hiel lost his family, from firstborn to youngest, in the course of rebuilding Jericho from its foundations to its gates (gates come last in the process of building a city), because the spring at Jericho, contaminated by contact with radioactive strata below, was affecting human fertility. According to the Deuteronomistic historian, the water was healed by Elisha, who threw salt (a symbol of cleansing) into the water; in fact, it is argued, the spring was purified by a further movement of the earth's crust, with the result that the water no longer flowed through radio-active strata. Whatever the reason, the historian's tradition is that the spring at Jericho became fit for human use again in the mid-ninth century BC, perhaps soon after the city's rebuilding by Hiel. This was a period of new life for Jericho.

We hear nothing of Jericho's inhabitants at this time, except for one particular group. Elijah and Elisha came to Jericho, where they met with 'the sons of the prophets who were at Jericho' (2 Kings 2:6; for a similar group at Bethel cf. 2 Kings 2:3). Their presence at Jericho may be due to the nearby important shrine of Gilgal (perhaps Khirbet Mefjar; cf. Amos 4:4; 5:5; Hos. 4:15; 9:12; 12:12). According to 1 Kings 2, the final parting of Elijah from Elisha took place after they had crossed the Jordan from Jericho eastward. After the event, Elisha recrossed the river, and began his career at Jericho (2 Kings 2:15 ff.) before going up into the hills to Bethel.

From this point on the Old Testament historians have very little to say about Jericho. A legend about Elisha's grave and its powers mentions that 'the Moabites used to invade the land in the spring of the year'; presumably their invasions affected particularly the Jericho area. When in the middle of the following century Jeroboam II of Israel (786–746 BC) 'restored the border of Israel from the entrance of Hamath as far as the sea of the Arabah', Jericho would have been the southernmost Israelite town west of the Jordan, but not so important that it deserved mention. According to 2 Chronicles 28:15, king Pekah of Israel (*c.* 737–732 BC) returned a number of Judaean captives to their brethren at Jericho, which suggests that Jericho was in Judahite territory at this point. Caution is necessary here, in view of the recent judgement that 'the narrative has little historical probability as it stands'.

When Israel became subject to Assyria in 721 BC, Jericho probably came under Assyrian administration. A century later, however, Jericho was probably incorporated into the kingdom of Judah by king Josiah (640–609 BC), if the city lists of Joshua 15:20–62; 18:21–28 belong, as has been argued, to this period. It is clear from 2 Kings 23:4 that Josiah's power extended north into at least part of what had been the kingdom of Israel. That Jericho was included is suggested by the discovery there of a stamped jar-handle, probably attributable to Josiah's reign and administration (see above p. 100). The last reference to Jericho in the pre-exilic period comes from the story of the collapse of Jerusalem before the Babylonian siege in 587 BC,

> Then a breach was made in the city; the king with all the men of war fled by night by the way of the gate between the two walls, by the king's garden, though the Chaldaeans were around the city. And they went in the direction of the Arabah. But the army of the Chaldaeans pursued the king, and overtook him in the plains of Jericho; and all his army were scattered from him (2 Kings 25:4f.).

The king and his officers were probably trying to escape to the kingdom of the Ammonites, which had also been involved in the rebellion against Babylon (cf. Ezek. 20:20; Jer. 40:14ff.). The same escape route was used later by Jason the high priest, ousted from Jerusalem in 171 BC (cf. 2 Macc. 4:26).

Jericho and its people are not now mentioned for nearly a century. This is hardly surprising, for we hear little of Judah between 587 BC and the resurrection of public life that followed the fall of Babylon to Cyrus the Persian in 539 BC. The first mention of Jericho comes in a list which has been variously interpreted as a record of those who returned to Judah from Babylon, a Persian taxation list, a list of Judaeans with rights to land in Judah, or a list of Judaeans with ancestral claims to be considered legitimate members of the post-exilic community. This list, however, of which there are three slightly varying versions (Ezra 2; Neh. 7; 1 Esdras 5), is a compilation of several groups of material. It contains lists of people by reference to their families (Ezra 2:3–20), or villages and towns (vv. 21–35), or their occupations (vv. 36–51), and a list of people whose pure Israelite ancestry and priestly origins were uncertified (vv. 59–62). 'The sons of Jericho' (Ezra 2:34) number 345, which compares interestingly with the numbers given for the other known places,

Gibbar (=Gibeon?)	95	Ramah and Geba	621
Bethlehem	123	Michmas	122
Netopah	56	Bethel and Ai	223
Anathoth	128	Nebo	52
(Beth) Azmaveth	42	Lod, Hadid, Ono	725
Kiriathaim, Chephirah, Beeroth	743		

The average number of sons for the seventeen places mentioned here is 187; Jericho has nearly twice as many. If 'sons' (perhaps originally 'men of') refers to the adult male population, we can perhaps reckon that Jericho had a total population of between 1000 and 1500 people. To precisely what date this refers is not easy to say. It depends upon the view taken of the purpose of the list. The fact that the list refers to people already dwelling in the various towns may suggest that it comes from the period after the initial political revival of Judah, perhaps the period after the work of Haggai and Zechariah (520–516 BC) when the temple is fully operative again (note the list's interest in temple personnel). It is also noteworthy that a large number of towns on this list belong, with Jericho, to the old Benjaminite territory – Anathoth, Kiriathaim, Beeroth, Ramah, Geba, Michmas, Bethel, Ai, Nebo (= Nob?), Lod, Hadid, Ono. It is possible that this list covers the area that was hardest hit by the deportations to Babylon in 587 BC and that it records the situation after restoration and resettlement at the end of the sixth century BC.

A later reference to Jericho occurs in the list of those who repaired the wall under Nehemiah in 444 BC, some sixty years after the situation depicted in the list of Ezra 2. The list in Nehemiah 3 shows that Judah, outside Jerusalem, contained at least the following towns – Jericho, Tekoa, Gibeon and Mizpah, Zanoah, Beth-hakkerem, Bethzur, and Keilah. There were many others; either they took no formal part in the work of rebuilding Jerusalem's walls, or their contribution was included under that of the nearest major town. Some of these towns were administrative centres for clearly defined districts – Jerusalem, Mizpah, Beth-hakkerem, Bethzur and Keilah (Jerusalem, Bethzur and Keilah were large enough to be divided into halves). Possibly Jericho and Tekoa also headed districts. The men of

Jericho, however, repaired the section of the wall next to the high priest and his family on the north side, somewhere between the Sheep Gate and the Fish Gate at the northeast and northwest corners of Jerusalem respectively (Neh. 3:2). Here the wall was particularly important, because the land rises towards the north, and the walls were not protected by any natural valleys and escarpments. Possibly the Jericho men worked here because this was the region of the old Benjamin Gate (Jer. 20:2; 37:13; 38:7; Zech. 14:10). Clearly the men of Jericho now felt that they belonged to the province of Judah and not to the provinces of Samaria or Ammon against whom Nehemiah was fortifying Jerusalem. This is further demonstrated by the discovery at Jericho of jar-handles stamped with the name of the province, *yhd*, and of the seal impression reading (?) *yhwd/'wryh*, especially if, as has been suggested, the Uriah named on it belonged to the family of Ezra's treasurer Meremoth (cf. Ezra 8:33).

In view of the location of the estates of Nehemiah's enemy Tobiah the Ammonite at Arak el-Emir a few miles across the Jordan from Jericho, the town may once again have become an important border post, though we hear nothing of any fortifications. On the whole Judah in the Persian period did not need fortified towns, at least while the Persian writ ran. But towards the end of the period, Judah may have experienced Persian displeasure. Eusebius says that Artaxerxes Ochus, campaigning against Egypt *c*. 350 BC, took captives from Judah and settled them near the Black Sea. Solinus (*c*. AD 260) says that 'Jerusalem was the head of Judaea, but it was destroyed; Jericho succeeded; and this city came to an end, destroyed in the war of Artaxerxes'. Solinus may be wrong about Jericho's moment of eminence and right about its final destruction. The evidence is far from secure, but the final years of the Persian empire certainly saw Persian campaigns in the Levant, and the book of Judith, with its description of the campaigns of general Holophernes, may have in mind a Cappadocian prince of that name who campaigned with Artaxerxes III in 341 BC. According to Judith 4:4, Jericho was one of the cities alerted and fortified against Holophernes. As the author of Judith appears to date this event soon after the exile, and combines in his narrative features from several hundred years of Israel's history, we cannot accept what he has to say at face value. But it was probably in the mid-fourth century BC that settled occupation on Tell es-Sultan came to an end. Pottery fragments from later periods have been found on the surface of the tell, but no remains of anything more permanent. This does not mean that the region became depopulated, but rather that people found it more convenient to live on a new site nearby.

For further reference

R. de Vaux, *The Early History of Israel*, 2 volumes, Darton, Longman and Todd, London, 1978.

M. Weippert, *The Settlement of the Israelite Tribes in Palestine*, Studies in Biblical Theology 2/21, S.C.M. Press, London, 1971.

M. Weippert and H. Weippert, 'Jericho in der Eisenzeit', *Zeitschrift des Deutschen Palästina-Vereins*, 92, Wiesbaden, 1976, pp. 105–148.

J. M. Miller and G. M. Tucker, *The Book of Joshua*, Cambridge Bible Commentary, Cambridge University Press, 1974.

J. Soggin, *Joshua: a commentary*, Old Testament Library, S.C.M. Press, London, 1972.

K. M. Kenyon, *The Archaeology of the Holy Land*, 4th edn., Benn, London; Norton, New York, 1979.

Y. Aharoni, *The Land of the Bible*, 2nd edn., Burns & Oates, London, 1979.

7

Jericho under the Hasmonaeans and the Herods

We are so used to seeing the land between the Jordan and the Mediterranean through biblical eyes that we might instinctively think of the history of Jericho in the biblical period as the history of Old Testament Jericho and New Testament Jericho. It is surprising how little Jericho appears in either Testament. Certainly, however, Jericho was an important place in the time of Jesus. Herod the Great had brought considerable splendour to Jericho by building his winter palace there, following the example set by the earlier Hasmonaean kings. But, partly for this reason and partly for the geographical reason which made Jericho so attractive to the wealthy, the Jericho region was something of a place apart, an oasis region on its own, separate from Jerusalem and probably politically and culturally aloof also. In some ways it had more in common with the semi-Hellenised regions east of the Jordan. This was perhaps also partly because it was an important town for travellers coming from Galilee and the Transjordan to Jerusalem; as is well known, Jewish travellers from Galilee used the Jordan valley route in preference to the direct route through Samaria.

In 331 BC Palestine and Transjordan changed their allegiance from Persia to Macedon as Alexander the Great marched south from Tyre. The recent discovery of a cave in Wadi Daliyeh a few miles north of Jericho, with its skeletons and papyrus documents, shows that certain people took refuge in the Jordan valley from Alexander and paid for it with their lives. In 312 BC southern Palestine and Transjordan were invaded by Ptolemy I of Egypt, and for the next century the region was under Egyptian administration. In 259 BC it was visited by an official called Zenon, the travelling agent of Apollonius, the minister of Ptolemy II Philadelphus, and there survive nearly forty papyrus documents relating to Zenon's journey. A fragment of his itinerary exists which shows that Zenon travelled from Strato's Tower on the Mediterranean coast to Jerusalem, thence to Jericho (where 5 *artabai* of wheat-flour were distributed among members of his party), and then across the Jordan to Abel Ha-shittim and the stronghold of Toubias at Arak el-Emir in the region of Ammanitis, about 13 miles (20 kms) from the Jordan fords near Jericho.

In 198 BC Jericho became, with the rest of Judah, part of the Seleucid empire, ruled from Antioch in Syria. The Seleucids inherited the Egyptian administration of the land and changed little, and Jericho's position probably remained much the same. Jericho's status in the final centuries BC is of some interest. We know that from the 2nd century BC onwards, Jericho was the haunt of royalty – Hasmonaeans, Herods, the Roman Antony and Egyptian Cleopatra – and the site of large royal estates. It has recently been speculated that

> the Jericho district already constituted a portion of the private domain of the ruler at the time of Alexander's conquest. It became the property of the conqueror and his heirs, being 'spear-won' land, according to Hellenistic custom. Consequently, the Jericho area was not urbanised and thus did not prejudice either the king's revenues or his estates. In any event, the flourishing of the oasis on a large scale can be connected with Hellenistic irrigation works (G. Foerster-G. Bacchi in *Encyclopedia of Archaeological Excavations in the Holy Land*, London, 1976, p. 565).

If the Jericho region under the Seleucids was virtually royal property, this may explain why there is no sign that the Maccabees, in their campaigns against the occupying Syrian power, derived any support from the Jericho region. Jericho is mentioned only twice in the Maccabaean period. Somewhere between April 160 BC and May 159 BC, Bacchides the Syrian general, trapped Jonathan and his men at the Jordan as they returned from a raid on the Madeba region (1 Macc. 9:43–49). Soon after this Bacchides

> built strong cities in Judaea: the fortress in Jericho, and Emmaus, and Beth-horon, and Bethel, and Timnath, and Pharathon, and Tephon, with high walls and gates and bars. And he placed garrisons in them to harass Israel (1 Macc. 9:50f.).

The phrase used suggests that the author has in mind not the town of Jericho but a small fort at Jericho. But the Maccabees probably took over the fort when Bacchides withdrew from Palestine in 147 BC. Sometime after 152 BC, when Jonathan assumed the rank of high priest (to which he was not strictly entitled), a group of men who objected to his action separated themselves from the Jerusalem temple and its cult and priesthood, and established themselves near Jericho on a small plateau at Qumran, away from the control of Jerusalem and far enough away from the Jericho oasis to be independent of it. (This was the beginnings of the community which produced the now famous 'Dead Sea Scrolls'.) In 134 BC Simon, now ruler of the independent Jewish state, was murdered at the fortress of Dok near Jericho (probably on or by the Mount of Temptation) by his son-in-law Ptolemy son of Abubus.

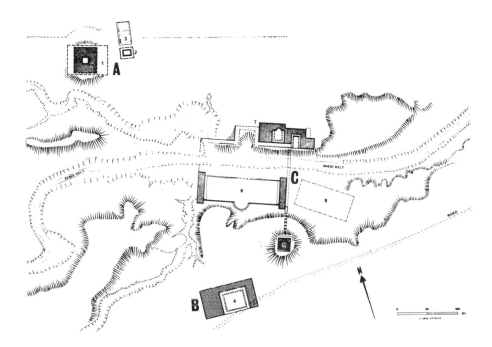

Figure 25 General plan of excavations at Tulul abu el-ᶜalaiq: A. Hasmonaean winter palace complex: 1. main building with later Herodian building (private royal villa?) on top (9); 2. pavillon; 3. swimming pool, promenade and colonnade. B. Herod's earlier winter palace on south bank. C. Herod's later palace: 5. southern mound with hall or bathhouse on top; 6. sunken garden; 7. northern wing; 8. swimming pool.

Ptolemy had been appointed 'commander for the plain of Jericho', which reveals that the oasis was thought of as a separate military area with its own administration. Ptolemy's name suggests that he was perhaps the grandchild of a man born when Judah was under Egyptian rule in the 3rd century BC; the name of his father, Abubus, is perhaps a Hellenised form of the Semitic name 'Beloved'. If Ptolemy was a local man, his attempted coup may reflect, as well as personal ambition, Jericho's sense of alienation from Jerusalem and the theocratic state centred on it. The old Jericho, on Tell es-Sultan, had belonged to Judah under the Persian empire and associated itself with Jerusalem. The affiliations of the new Jericho had probably been rather with the Ptolemaic and then the Seleucid administrations than with Jerusalem (especially if the oasis had been regarded as the private estate of the Ptolemaic and Seleucid kings). Jericho was not situated in the region of Judah from which the Maccabees derived most of their support, and it probably did not have much sympathy with them.

117

However, Ptolemy's attempted coup failed, and Simon's son John Hyrcanus besieged Ptolemy in Dok, from which Ptolemy fled to Philadelphia (Amman). Hyrcanus went on to capture a large amount of territory in Transjordan, and later Alexander Jannaeus (103–76 BC) added to it by taking the fortresses of Gadara and Amathus, and subduing the people of Gilead and Moab. For all this control of Jericho was necessary, and doubtless the Hasmonaeans saw that it was well garrisoned. But while Jericho's essential non-Jewishness may have caused some military difficulty, the same factor made it attractive to the Hasmonaean monarchy and its successors as a refuge from the political problems of Jerusalem. Excavations at Tulul abu el-ᶜalaiq since 1973 have shown that the mound on the north side of the Wadi Qelt was originally built, probably by Jannaeus, as a winter-palace complex, extending altogether over about three acres (Figure 25). There was a large central building 52 × 48 m, with a colonnaded swimming pool surrounded by a promenade, with further buildings to the east. An aqueduct brought water from ᶜAin Duk and ᶜAin Nuᶜeima to this pool and to a complex of bathing installations added later. Coloured frescoes were found in the palace dating from the reigns of Jannaeus and Aristobulus (from whom Herod the Great took over in 37 BC). This was the pleasure resort of the Hasmonaean kings; it was not the town of Jericho, which lay about 2 kms east, probably on the site of modern Jericho.

Hasmonaean interest in this area can be seen from other sites. Hyrcanus built the fort of Hyrcania in the wilderness east-south-east of Jerusalem, and Jannaeus extended the fort of Alexandreion, situated on a hill north of Jericho. Across the Dead Sea was Machaerus where, according to Josephus, John the Baptist was executed. The enemy in mind was probably the Nabataeans, whose kings Obodas and Aretas each defeated Jannaeus, in north-east Transjordan and near Lydda respectively.

Jericho featured on a number of occasions during the political struggles of the Hasmonaean dynasty. Jannaeus' successor and widow, Salome Alexandra, ruled while their sons Hyrcanus and Aristobulus grew up; on her death in 67 BC their rivalry became war. The younger Aristobulus defeated Hyrcanus at Jericho and besieged him in Jerusalem. Hyrcanus surrendered and retired, but later with Nabataean help reopened the struggle. They besieged Aristobulus in Jerusalem. At this point the Roman general Pompey arrived in Syria to assert Roman rule in place of the now collapsed Seleucid kingdom. Both Hyrcanus and Aristobulus appealed to Pompey, who moved into Judaea via the Jordan valley, stopping a night at Jericho. Eventually, after a three month siege of Jerusalem, Pompey took Aristobulus to Rome to show him off in his triumphal procession, leaving Hyrcanus as high priest in Jerusalem. Jericho and the Hasmonaean fortresses round about had in

Plate 20   Swimming pool on the northern mound of Herodian Jericho.

fact been totally unable to prevent the Roman army marching up to Jerusalem. The Jericho region was the Achilles' heel of Judaea; as George Adam
Smith pointed out, Jericho could easily be cut off by an army occupying the
hills above it to the west. In 57–55 BC, after some resistance by Aristobulus'
son Alexander, the Roman general Gabinius demolished the fortresses of
Alexandreion, Hyrcania and Machaerus, and divided the Jewish nation into
five *sunodoi*, unions, whose administrative centres were Jerusalem, Gazara,
Amathus, Jericho, and Sepphoris. Judaea itself was thus divided into three
units, Gazara in the west, Jerusalem in the middle, and Jericho in the east.
Again Jericho was recognised as an area quite separate from Jerusalem,
though a few years later Gabinius reunited these areas under the authority
of the high priest Hyrcanus.

When Pompey, under whose authority these arrangements were made,
was murdered in 48 BC, Hyrcanus and his Idumaean supporter Antipater
turned to Julius Caesar, who made Antipater a Roman citizen and procurator
of Judaea. Antipater in turn gave his sons Phasael and Herod administrative
charge of Judaea and Galilee respectively. Antipater was killed in a con-
spiracy, and Herod rapidly established himself as the main power in the
land; in 40 BC he was appointed king of Judaea by Antony and the Senate
in Rome. By 37 BC he had ousted Antigonus, who was his rival for the
throne and Hyrcanus' rival for the high-priesthood.

Jericho played a part in these events. Herod used it as a source of supplies
in his war against Antigonus; on one occasion he looted it, and left a garrison
there. On another, he dined at Jericho with the local magistrates; after

dinner, when all had left, the building collapsed. In the morning, Herod and his party were attacked from the hills and Herod received a javelin wound. His two charmed escapes brought him new supporters: 'multitudes of Jews now joined him from Jericho and elsewhere', says Josephus.

Clearly Herod liked Jericho. He was not a Jerusalem Jew, and his various building achievements outside Jerusalem – at Samaria, Caesarea and elsewhere, even outside Palestine – show his taste for the Hellenistic world. He used the Hasmonaean winter palace – among other things – for the murder in 35 BC of his brother-in-law, the high priest Aristobulus, who, according to Josephus, 'was sent by night to Jericho, and there, in accordance with Herod's instructions, plunged into a swimming bath by the Gauls and drowned'. The bath has been identified with the large swimming pool east of the central building on the northern mound at Tulul abu el-ᶜalaiq (see Plate 20). But Herod was soon deprived of Jericho, for in 34 BC Antony gave Jericho, together with the coast of Palestine, to Cleopatra; the particular attraction was the revenue from the balsam groves. Herod rented the area back from Cleopatra at 200 talents per annum, and after the defeat of Antony and Cleopatra at Actium in 31 BC regained it for himself. Josephus tells us that 'above Jericho he built the walls of a fortress, remarkable alike for its solidity and beauty, which he dedicated to his mother under the name of Kypros' (*B.J.*1.417). This tower is now located at the top of a hill south of Herod's palace, and excavation there in 1974 showed that beneath it was an earlier Hasmonaean fort (perhaps either the Threx or Taurus mentioned as forts by Strabo, *Geog.*xvi.2.40). Josephus also notes that,

> at Jericho, between the fortress of Cypros and the former palace [i.e. the Hasmonaean palace on the north side of the Wadi Qelt], the king constructed new buildings, finer and more commodious for the reception of guests, and named them after the same friends [i.e. Augustus and Agrippa] (*B.J.* 1.407; Loeb translation).

Herod's building on the site was apparently in two stages. First he built a winter palace on the south bank, back from the wadi bed, consisting of a large central court, with a columned hall on one side and a series of small rooms, two containing stepped baths, on the north and east sides. Towards the end of his reign, Herod built a new palace which straddled the Wadi Qelt. Prominent on the south bank of the wadi is the 'southern mound', which was formed by pouring a fill of earth round the foundations of a building; this formed the platform for the building on top – probably a bathhouse. From this building at the top of the mound, a flight of stairs ran northwards down to the wadi. To the right lay a large swimming pool (40 × 92 m), but to the left an enormous sunken garden, running west-east,

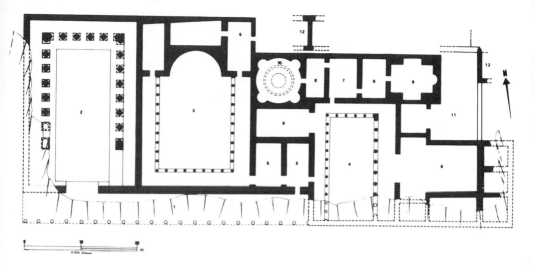

Figure 26   Plan of northern wing of Herod's palace: 1. portico facing wadi; 2.
large paved hall; 3. court with Ionic columns; 4. court with Corinthian
columns: 7. *apodyterium* (undressing room); 8. *tepidarium* (warm bath
room); 9. *caldarium* (hot bath room); 10. *frigidarium* (cold bath room).

with a double colonnade at each end. The southern wall had on the inside
a row of niches built in the Roman style of brickwork known as *opus
reticulatum* ('network'), in which concrete masonry is lined with small,
square-faced pyramidal blocks set at a 45° angle. The niches, about 1 m
wide and ½ m deep, were alternately semi-circular and rectangular recesses;
25 were placed each side of an *exedra*, a semi-circular series of terraces
extending up the hill, with a water basin (still water-proof when found) at
the bottom, and flowerpots on the terraces. The garden was 113.67 m long;
its northern wall (which has almost entirely disappeared) ran along the south
bank of the wadi.

The steps down from the southern mound probably continued across the
wadi by a bridge to the northern wing of this palace complex. Here the main
buildings were mostly of mud-brick. At the west end is a great reception
hall, or *triclinium*, 19 × 29 m, with columns round the inside of three walls,
the fourth being open to the south and the view across to the sunken garden.
The floor had been paved with imported marble and local coloured stone,
with a mosaic panel in the middle. The two main rows of columns were
13 m apart, and must have been spanned by enormous beams, probably
imported cypress. In the centre of the building was an apsed hall or court
with Ionic columns; the eastern wing was another, smaller hall or court
with Corinthian columns. On the northeast corner was a bathhouse with a
frigidarium (Figure 26).

Further to the west, the remains of the original Hasmonaean palace on the 'northern mound' were covered by a small building of which only some fragments of decorative stucco and walls remain. It was perhaps Herod's private villa, with immediate access to the swimming pool just to its east. Excavations in 1976 east of this villa and pool uncovered the remains of a Hasmonaean building, later covered by Herodian gardens, and also a house, perhaps two-storeyed, with a frescoed central hall, which was interpreted as the main living quarters of the Herodian palace complex.

This magnificent collection of buildings, with clear traces of Roman architecture and workmanship, was probably built during the last decade of Herod's life (13–4 BC). The Roman influence is interesting, as Herod did not build like this elsewhere, but Jericho, in the valley bottom, had always built in brick rather than stone. The *opus reticulatum* belongs to the Augustan period, and Herod may have brought the idea back with him from his visits to Rome. Some have suggested that it was not Herod but his son Archelaus (4 BC–AD 6) who built this palace, for Josephus says that Archelaus sumptuously rebuilt Herod's palace which had been destroyed by his slave Simeon (*Ant.* 17.10.6; 17.13.1). But there is no trace of any destruction, and Josephus does not specify how much rebuilding Archelaus did. It is probably best to suppose that the palace layout is basically Herod's work.

These were not the only Herodian buildings at Jericho. According to Josephus, there were also a hippodrome and an amphitheatre, both of which have recently been tentatively located at Tell es-Sammarat. Before his death, Herod had the notables of Judaea locked into the hippodrome and ordered their massacre at his death. When he died in Jericho five days later, his death was announced in the amphitheatre, and his body was taken to the Herodeion, the fortress Herod had prepared as his tomb five miles east-south-east of Bethlehem. In the half-century after Herod's death, the palaces seem to have decayed; after AD 6 Judaea had no king (apart from the short reign of Agrippa, AD 41–44), and the Roman prefects like Pontius Pilate ruled Judaea from Caesarea on the Mediterranean coast and probably preferred to take their holidays out of Palestine altogether.

If the palaces decayed, however, the local town remained. In the gospels we hear the story of the man who went down from Jerusalem to Jericho, the account of Jesus' meeting and dining with the chief tax-collector Zacchaeus, and of the blind beggar Bartimaeus sitting by the road. Jericho was a staging post and administrative centre, an inevitable centre for travellers, taxmen and beggars. Under Roman administration, Jericho was one of the three toparchies of south-eastern Judah, along with Engaddi and Herodium, which lay to its south and southwest respectively. To the north of the toparchy of Jericho lay Gophna. Thus the Jericho toparchy was restricted to the Jericho

Plate 21   Roman pottery and glass of the first century AD, Jericho.

plain west of the Jordan; it probably reached as far as Phasaelis and Archelais to the north and Ras Feshka, the promontory jutting out into the Dead Sea just below Qumran, on the south.

The region of Jericho is not mentioned in the New Testament outside the gospels and Hebrews 11:30, and there is no evidence that the first generation of Christian evangelists preached there. This is perhaps surprising, and it may be that what preaching there was passes unmentioned because no Christian community arose as a result of it. Jericho appears again in its usual role in the course of the great Jewish revolt of AD 66–70. When the Roman general Vespasian set about crushing it, he secured Galilee and the north first, and from Caesarea on the coast he crossed to Peraea in Transjordan and secured Gadara (modern es-Salt?). He then secured the western approaches, and marched via Samaria to Jericho and joined the force from Peraea. According to Josephus,

The mass of the population, anticipating their arrival, had fled from Jericho to the hill country over against Jerusalem, but a considerable number remained behind and were put to death; the city itself the Romans found deserted . . . Vespasian, with a view to investing Jerusalem on all sides, now established camps at Jericho and Adida, placing in each a garrison composed jointly of Romans and auxiliaries (*B.J.* 4.451, 486; Loeb translation).

123

The aim of these garrisons, probably drawn mainly from the tenth legion, was not defence so much as blockade. Vespasian now had a firm military grasp of all the main routes to and from Jerusalem. Jericho was important to the Jews as a possible escape route from Jerusalem, as it had been on similar occasions in the past, and to the Romans as a base for supplies from the fertile Jordan valley. Vespasian himself took the opportunity while at Jericho of visiting the Dead Sea, and to test its strange reputation,

> ordered certain persons who were unable to swim to be flung into the deep water with their hands tied behind them; with the result that all rose to the surface and floated, as if impelled upward by a current of air (*B.J.* 4.477; Loeb translation).

It was perhaps also at this point that Khirbet Qumran was destroyed, for the latest Jewish coins found in the layer of destruction there were put into circulation in Nisan, AD 68, and the earliest Roman coins from the level above the destruction layer date from AD 67–68. These coins were coins of Caesarea and Dor, coastal cities in whose coinage the Roman soldiers received their pay, and they come from a level which marks the existence of the Roman military post which was established after the capture of the site.

When Vespasian returned to Rome to become emperor in AD 69, leaving his son Titus in charge of the siege of Jerusalem, Titus ordered the tenth legion to come up to Jerusalem via Jericho, after putting a garrison there to guard the pass, and it converged on Jerusalem with the fifth legion from Emmaus and the twelfth and fifteenth legions from Caesarea. Jerusalem fell in September, AD 70, but surprisingly the forts which surrounded the Jericho region remained in Jewish hands – Herodeion, Machaerus, and Masada. Lucretius Bassus took Herodeion easily; Machaerus accepted the offer of free withdrawal for the defenders. L. Flavius Silva finally took Masada after a determined siege and fierce resistance in AD 73. After Masada fell, the Roman garrison was probably withdrawn from Qumran a few miles north of Masada, for there are no coins datable after AD 72–73.

How deeply these events affected Jericho is not known. The destruction of the Jerusalem temple may not have moved the local population much. The region will have continued to be part of the imperial province of Judaea. Perhaps there were more veteran Roman soldiers settled on the land round Jericho, as at Emmaus and Shechem. Jericho would continue its ancient role as a staging post between Judaea and the Transjordanian provinces, especially the kingdom of Nabataea, based on Petra, which became a Roman province in AD 106. It was not long before Jericho became a stopping point for a new kind of traveller, the Christian pilgrim, as he tried to follow the roads once taken by his master, with results that we have already seen.

For further reference

J. Finegan, *The Archaeology of the New Testament*, Princeton University Press, 1969.

J. D. Kelso and D. C. Baramki, *Excavations at New Testament Jericho and Khirbet en-Nitla*, Annual of the American Schools of Oriental Research, 29–30 (1949–51), New Haven, 1955.

J. B. Pritchard, *The Excavations at Herodian Jericho (1951)*, Annual of the American Schools of Oriental Research, 32–33 (1952–4), New Haven, 1958.

E. Netzer, 'The winter palaces of the Judaean kings at Jericho at the end of the Second Temple period', *Bulletin of the American Schools of Oriental Research*, 228 (1977) 1–13.

Josephus, *Jewish War* and *Antiquities*, Loeb edition, edited by H. St. J. Thackeray, R. Marcus, A. Wikgren, L. H. Feldman, Harvard University Press, 1956–1965.

M. Avi-Yonah, *Map of Roman Palestine*, Oxford University Press, London, 1940.

Indexes

General

Aharoni, Y. 98, 114
Albright, W. F. 33, 76
Amiran, R. 63, 67, 80
Ammonites 109, 111
Amorites 77, 81f, 84, 88
Anati, E. 45, 54, 63
Anatolia 67, 70f
Antony 116, 120
Arak el-emir 113, 115
archaeology at Jericho 29–36
Aristobulus, high priest 120
Assyrians 30, 111
animals 17f, 38, 42, 47f, 50, 59, 81, 100

Babylonians 30, 111
balm, balsam 18, 20f, 120
Baramki, D. C. 35
Bartimaeus 122
Beersheba 66–69
Beidha 47f, 50, 52, 56
Beisamun 48, 56f
Benjamin, tribe of 106–8, 112
burials 38, 40, 52, 61, 64, 66, 78–80, 83, 89–96, 100
Byblos 56–58, 83

civilization 46
clothes 91
Condor, C. R. 30, 36
copper 70f, 78
Cypros (fortress) 120

David 24, 108f
Dead Sea 12, 17–19, 22, 24, 37, 124
deforestation 76
Deuteronomistic historian 102–107, 110
Dorrell, P. 42f

Egypt 69, 81–88, 93, 95f, 98, 109, 115–117
Elijah 24, 110
Elisha 11, 24, 27, 110
epigraphic material 68, 82, 97, 100, 102, 111, 113
erosion 47, 76, 93, 97
Eynan 38
Execration texts 82
Exodus 32–34

figurines 50, 57f
flints 32, 37f, 40, 42, 47, 57, 59, 62, 71
flora 18–24
food 20f, 37f, 40–42, 44, 46–48, 59, 81, 88, 91
furniture 90f

Garstang, J. 31–34, 46, 54–57, 63, 75, 89, 96, 98, 100
geology 11, 14, 16
Gilgal 104, 106, 108, 110

Habiru 32, 86–88
Herod the Great 35, 115, 118–122
Hiel 106, 109f
houses 42, 44, 46–48, 50, 52, 59f, 78, 88, 97f, 100
Hyksos 84, 86, 93

Israelites 93, 96, 99–114

Jericho: Natufian 37–39, 42; 'proto-Neolithic' 40; PPNA 32, 34f, 40–47, 49f; PPNB 47–54; Pottery Neolithic A and B 56–62; Chalcolithic 60–62, 67; Ghassulian 61f; Proto-urban 64–68; EB 33f, 68–76, 78; Intermediate EB–MB 34, 76–83; MB 20, 30, 33, 76f, 83–96, 106; LB 31–34, 96–98; Iron Age 98–114; Persian Period 100, 102, 111–113; Hellenistic Age 115; Hasmonaean 115–118, 122; Herodian 28, 35, 118–122; Roman 30, 35, 119, 122–124; later periods 30
Jerusalem 24, 68f. 82, 105, 112, 117–119, 124
Josephus 11, 14, 19, 120, 123, 124f
Joshua 25, 27, 30, 96, 98f, 102–107; book of Joshua, 102–107
Judah 111–113, 116f

Kebaran culture 37f
Kelso, J. 35, 125
Kenyon, K. M. 30–36, 40, 46, 48, 50, 52, 55f, 58, 60, 63, 66f, 76, 78, 80, 83, 88f, 94–97, 109, 114
Kitchener, H. H. 30, 36

Maccabees 116f
Madeba map 25

Biblical References